UNDER THE
INFLUENCE OF
EVIL

UNDER THE INFLUENCE OF EVIL

A BRUTALLY ABUSIVE CHILDHOOD EXPOSED

DARLENE DEACON

Dedication

This book is dedicated to the millions of boys and girls, men and women worldwide who have suffered abuse at the hands of the people who were supposed to love and protect them. The long lasting, sometimes life sentences of suffering, can be, to some degree, overcome with hard work and brutal self-honesty.

I wish I could put my arms around all of you and make the pain go away, but it is not that easy. It is up to us to become the people we want to be. Blaming our past, or our abusers, is not productive. Unfortunately, we have to find the answers within ourselves and succumb to therapy or a strong dedication to self-help and honest self-evaluation study. Be strong. You always have, or you wouldn't be reading this. Be brave and unafraid to look inside and see the broken places that need your love and attention. Once you start caring about yourself, your life will begin to change, and the healing will begin. The work is a tiring and lifelong commitment, but most "normal" people never take the time to work on such in-depth self-improvement because it isn't as obvious a need as ours is. We have the blessings of knowing we need to identify our deficits, grow, heal, and ultimately become the best we can be.

Table of Contents

Throughout this book you will find words in **bold**; they are explained in the Glossary. I've also included an Index for easy referencing.

Acknowledgements

Author Sally J. Ling, thank you for your constructive criticism that helped me transform this manuscript into what it is today.

Thank you, Author and Poet Laureate of Vermont, Sydney Lea, for your compassion, understanding, and invaluable advice.

Marion Romano, cousin, I cannot thank you enough for all the tedious reading and editing. I will forever love you for your sweet adoration and the laughs you gave me through the rough moments of re-reading my past.

Kathi Milicia for your tender compassion and your fiery red pen in the final proofreading and editing of this manuscript. I am so grateful for your work, but mostly your precious friendship.

Virginia Graceffa, my dear aunt, I thank you for the insight and information that no one else could provide because so few were there who are willing to tell it and I was way too young to remember.

And lastly, I'd like to thank "Tiny" for your willingness to admit, that not only you were there, but that you participated in the sex "parties" my mother initiated, and then share those stories and the details of other events that were often too horrid for me to remember fully.

Introduction - Handwritten by my Aunt

My Aunt Jo was still a bit shaken when she gave me this note—well, actually she insisted upon rewriting it after I asked her if I could use it as my introduction. She was embarrassed since she had made so many grammatical errors in her emotional state. I was so moved by her words that I had to share it with you. I like the original better, but I had to respect her wishes.

Dear Darlene,

I finished your book with tears in my eyes. I wish I had known all you were going through all those years. I would like to have been able to take you away from Lester and your mother even not knowing all you were going thru, I knew from your looks and behavior you were down trodden. My son, Frankie, first bloody lips was because some boy called you a whore and he punched him. I gave him the devil for fighting, but he never told me why. I feel one of my biggest failures in life is not trying harder to help you.

I called your mother and
told her to take care of
you and George or I would
take you away from her.
She came to our house and
had a gun on her hip
and said she would
shoot our whole family if
I tried. My husband
told me to stay out of it
before she came here drunk

and shot us all. So I
backed away. I was
afraid of her.

I'm so sorry.

Love your, aunt
Ginny

1 - I'll Kill You

I was just waking up. The dull, metallic, clunking sound as I shifted my legs and the old, thin rug scraping my bare skin reminded me of where I was—chained to the floor, again. I sat up and looked around. Dick had already gone to work.

Like any normal person in the morning, I had to pee. I wondered how long I'd have to wait for him to come back, so I turned around to see what time it was. He'd taken the clock. I was horrified.

MY GOD, HE DOESN'T EVEN WANT ME TO KNOW WHAT TIME IT IS.

I sat and waited. As the hours passed, my bladder began to scream. I thought about my options:

I COULD YELL FOR HELP... BUT HE MIGHT COME HOME... FOR LUNCH... I DON'T' KNOW WHAT TIME IT IS... I DON'T EVEN KNOW HOW LONG I'VE BEEN HERE... AND IF HE HEARS ME YELLING... HE'LL BE MAD.

I looked at the key that went to the padlock on my ankle; he'd hung it on the wall above the radiator.

I WONDER IF I CAN REACH IT...

I stood up and dragged the chain as far as it would go and then stretched my arm and body toward the key. A part of me was afraid to touch it; he'd trained me well and this was strictly taboo. But the pressure in my bladder was intensifying, and I only hesitated for a moment.

I could just barely touch the tip of the key with the end of my forefinger. I stretched farther as the chain dug more painfully into my ankle bones. I couldn't quite squeeze the key between the tips of my two fingers.

IF I DROP THAT KEY, THERE'S NO WAY I'LL BE ABLE TO GET IT FROM BEHIND THAT BIG, OLD RADIATOR WITH THIS CHAIN ON... AND IF HE COMES HOME AND FINDS OUT I TRIED TO UNLOCK MYSELF...HE'LL WHIP THE HELL OUT OF ME.

I slumped to the floor and rubbed my sore ankle:

THIS IS GETTING BAD... HE'S NEVER LEFT ME HERE ALL DAY BEFORE.

I'd just turned 16.

I didn't get into this situation overnight; it took a little coaxing, but believe it or not, things were actually worse before I got here. Not many people knew how bad it was, but the ones who did, still don't want this story told. My mother is one of them.

"I'll kill you if you hurt the family with that book!" It was her first response without any hesitation. I often wondered—and still do—if she'd have followed through with her threat. With the safety of thousands of miles between us, however, I continued writing despite my fear of her.

I began by jotting down my thoughts and feelings about my painful life. Those little scribblings led to a fierce obsession to continue writing. It soon became therapeutic and the more I wrote, the more I had to write.

Some people can't fathom the fact that children live through such a myriad of traumatic experiences. Maybe it's because not many survive well enough to tell their stories, but I did. Now, more than two decades later, I am ready to bring you on a journey I hope will change your perspective on life and the true meaning of challenge.

2 - Daddy, Why Do We do This?

The abuse and resulting damage started long before I can remember. Even as early as my first day of school, I can remember how much I hated to leave my mother home alone. I couldn't help feeling guilty as I left her standing there at the bus stop. I'd been taking care of her in one way or another for several years already, and I felt like going to school as just another one of my adult-like responsibilities, like going to work I suppose. It was June of 1969. I was six years old.

I liked school, but I can't remember much about my friends or activities. I do remember the night when Dad was standing by his bureau, undressing. I was sitting on my parent's bed; I was naked.

Mom was probably out bar hopping again, which gave Dad the perfect opportunity to be alone with me and practice his perversion; something he did whenever Mom was out. We'd been doing this for so long that it seemed perfectly normal to me.

I don't remember the whole conversation that night, but he made me feel flattered and that I was exclusive to him. We were talking about my "privates" again. That was the only thing I'd ever called them. He said, "Daddy's the only one who can touch them."

During our naked times together, sometimes Dad said the most ridiculous things as he coaxed me into doing what he wanted. This time, we were sitting on his bed when he said, "Maybe someday you can lick it and suck it like Mommy does."

I was stunned and I scrunched my face all up and said, "She does that?" I couldn't believe my mother would do such a silly thing. I figured he was lying just to get me to do it.

Finally, I blurted out, "Daddy, why do we do this?"

He said, "Because I love you, that's why, but you can never tell Mommy or we won't be able to do it anymore."

A sickening feeling went through me. I remember feeling angry because he assumed I wanted to do it and angrier with myself because I didn't dare tell him how I felt.

For many years into my adulthood, I blamed all my problems on sexual abuse. I didn't know I'd been abused in several ways since I was an infant and by more than just the two people I called my parents.

A much older cousin filled me in on some of the things that had happened when I was an infant. She said I was less than a year-and-a-half old when my mother came home from work to find my unemployed father in a drunken sleep. Apparently, I was running around the apartment without a diaper. Mom told my cousin about it, who later told me, when she went to put a diaper on me, she found a crayon in my vagina. Then, she told me with a great deal of disgust, my mother said I did it to myself.

I also learned, from several sources, my mother had physically abused me from the time I was an infant. I've heard countless stories about her violent temper during those early years, but this story seemed to stick out in several people's minds.

It was one of Mom's countless jealous rampages when she kicked the television so hard she broke the screen. She was angry with my father because he was watching a show with good-looking women in it. Magazines, newspapers, or anything with images of pretty women often sent her into a rage.

Mom often became violently angry with the smallest of things. I remember feeling frightened anytime she showed the slightest sign of displeasure. When I felt afraid, I knew that I had to stifle my own feelings and try to evaluate hers. Then, I'd try to figure out what to do, what to say, or how to act that would most likely prevent her from becoming more upset. It was my way of deflecting her anger away from me since I usually became the target. Nonetheless, I'd always felt frightened, and thought it was just part of life, a normal feeling.

I began to respond to both my parents and everyone else purely out of fear. This is **co-dependent** behavior, and it was just the beginning of mine.

As I rehashed the horrid events of my life on these pages, I began to understand why I was afraid to make simple choices that would have little or no effect on anything; like which bottle and brand of ketchup to buy at the grocery store. I had no emotional independence, so I was afraid to express my feelings—even simple laughter—without some kind of permission or sign that it was okay. It may seem ridiculous, but this was my world. Eventually, I was able to understand better why I felt guilty about nearly everything, including my first day of school when I left my mother home alone.

3 - Game of Love

There were signs of mental illness and instability when, my mother, Jean, was a young girl. She was the younger of two daughters. Her sister, Jo-Ann (Aunt Jo), was two years older.

"You don't know the abuse I've had to put up with through the years—since I was very young—because of your mother's meanness and actions—[it was] embarrassing and shameful even as a young girl." My aunt's voice still harbored signs of fear and pain as she told me this at age of 70.

Darlene before head injury

My mother's jealousy and competitiveness about everything was fierce. Her sister was the first and closest competitor and the target of the resulting anger and bitterness. It became more intense as the years passed, and eventually no one was exempt from my mother's deep-seeded jealousy.

Both girls were very pretty. Mom had gorgeous strawberry-blonde hair, blue eyes, and a great build. Still, she was viciously jealous of Aunt Jo, her marriage and children.

The two women became pregnant just weeks apart in 1961. This would be my mother's first child and my aunt's second.

Aunt Jo and Uncle Tony already had a three-year-old son, Craig. Mom wanted to have a boy, too and always had.

Much to her disappointment, I, a girl, was born in the summer of 1962. Then, to add insult to Mom's psychological injury, Aunt Jo gave birth to their second son five weeks later. Many times over the years, Mom told me how much she'd wanted a son instead of a daughter.

From what I understand, Mom couldn't afford to pay someone to watch me during the day while she worked. I stayed with my aunt and uncle in the suburbs of Boston during the week and visited with Mom on weekends. It may have saved my life since Mom had no trouble admitting that she abused me.

I was no different from any other infant. I squirmed and wiggled when my mother changed my diaper and she had no patience for that kind of irritation. So, she beat my legs with a brush in an attempt to make me stop. She admitted it when Aunt Jo asked why I had so many bruises on my legs. "Isn't that a little rough?" My aunt asked. Mom callously said, "She was driving me crazy." I was about 16 months old when Mom brought me back to my aunt's house with six stitches in my head. She claims I fell down a flight of stairs.

Not long after that, Mom said I hit my head on my crib and ripped open the same wound. There are few, if any pictures for a year or so after that, and then I wore bangs to cover the scar. It eventually healed and turned into a hefty scar on my forehead that's still too wide to look like a wrinkle at the age of 53.

Ironically, Mom often told people that my aunt beat her kids with the implication she beat me, too. For a while, a lot of people believed her since, back then, I always had so many bruises on my body. My mother also accused various other people of ridiculous things over the years, but Aunt Jo and Uncle Tony seemed to be a constant target of her accusations and lies. After many years of witnessing my mother doing the same things she accused other people of doing, I realized she was actually describing her own feelings and actions. I'm sure she was trying to draw attention away from herself.

I was almost four years old when Mom and Dad bought their first home in Massachusetts. It was a nice ranch-style house in a middle class neighborhood. It had a big yard and lots of woods behind the house for me to play in and cranberry bogs next to the house with lots of trails and sandpits.

Though I finally went to live with Mom and Dad all the time, I remember feeling very uncomfortable and shy around Dad. I guess I hadn't seen much of him, so I hardly knew him. My father is six feet tall with dark-brown, curly hair, and glasses.

Meanwhile, my mother's competitive nature didn't end with her own battle to be the best. Apparently, I was in direct competition with my younger cousin from the day he was born. Mom became obsessed with making me learn everything first and fastest. She also demanded explicit obedience whether her orders were right or wrong. She insisted on having the best-behaved and smartest child of all the children she knew, especially her sister's.

I know now, this really had nothing to do with me. It had to do with the fact that Mom believed my behavior and mental acuity reflected directly on her. This obsession would later drive her to extremes.

My oldest cousin, Craig, remembers one of her over-zealous methods when he was visiting us at our new house. He was watching while Mom taught me how to count. I'd count out loud for her, but each time I made a mistake, she'd slap me across the face. Then she'd make me start over again. I was three years old and Craig was six, and it upset him terribly. He told his mother he didn't want to visit us anymore after that. I don't remember it at all, but I have no doubt this was one of the many twisted ways she taught me how to be afraid of making mistakes of any kind—a fear I carried long into my adulthood.

It wasn't long after we moved into our new house when Mom and Dad played a bizarre game with me, which I've never forgotten. First, Mom told me to go stand in the hallway while they sat at opposite ends of the kitchen table. I could see Dad through the doorway, but not Mom at the other end of the table. Then, both of them started calling my name, "Darlene, come to Mamma"—"No, Darlene come to Daddy." I was confused and scared:

WHICH ONE OF THEM AM I SUPPOSED TO RUN TO?

I ran to Mom every time, mostly out of fear. I couldn't reject her that way because I'd pay for it somehow. I'll admit it was fun the first few times, because Mom hugged me lavishly, gave me an abundance of praise, and told me I was a "good girl." After a while, I realized my choice hurt Dad's feelings. I wanted to run to him, just to make him feel better, but I was afraid. I didn't know why.

We played this stupid game until I became sick of it because Mom always won. I started to feel angry. Somehow, I knew she was only doing it to hurt Dad. I felt guilty because I was the one really hurting him.

In an attempt to make up for hurting his feelings, I mustered up the courage to run to him. Like my mother, I thought I had to "show" him I loved him, too. I ran toward him, but pulled up short, afraid to move. I just stood there with my head down. Suddenly, I felt terribly uncomfortable, so I quickly turned away and ran to Mom again. I now felt worse for hurting him again.

This game of love had an enormous impact on me. I was about four years old, and as young as I was, I recognized my mother's sadistic nature, although I didn't know the words to describe it then. What I was able to understand was how my mother seemed to get some sort of satisfaction from the obvious way the rejection affected Dad. She had to prove to him, and I suspect, to herself as well that "I loved her most."

There were so many bizarre things that had happened in my young life already. So far, this next one remains in the top five on the list. Obviously, Mom never had much patience with me. I had to go to the bathroom and was still small enough that Mom had to lift me onto the toilet seat. I had to hold myself up with both hands to keep from falling in. She sat on the tub waiting and I could sense her growing impatience, which didn't help me get the job done any faster. Well, as far as she was concerned, I was done. Without giving me a chance to object, she lifted me from the seat. Well, my "poop" landed on the floor. I was horrified thinking I was in deep do-do. Much to my amazement, she seemed interested instead of angry. Mom had noticed some undigested corn in the poop and decided to give me a biology lesson.

She told me to wait and she trundled off to the kitchen while I cleaned myself up. She brought back a knife and saucer. I held my breath, wondering what she was going to do. She picked up the poop, put it on the saucer and began slicing it up so I could examine the undigested corn up-close. It was disgusting, but I knew I had to act as if I was extremely interested so she wouldn't get upset. I don't remember anything after that.

On a lighter note...

In the summertime, we vacationed in Down East Maine where my mother was born and raised. We stayed with my grandparents in Grand Lake Stream, a beautiful tiny town fondly known as "Grand Lake." The year-round population is still only about 150 people (2015). The entire region has an abundance of lakes, rivers, and streams.

My grandfather was a hunting and fishing guide and my grandmother was a cook for the sportsmen. They were hard-working, exceptional people.

While we were there, we always visited my great-grandfather who lived in a cabin in the middle of the woods on a lake. The only way to get to the cabin is by an unpaved, logging road. To date, there is no electricity or running water and gaslights, outhouses, and gas generators are still used when necessary.

My great-grandfather was a tall, strong, but gentle man. I remember sitting on his lap by the lakeshore next to the campfire as a child. I was a thin kid with snow white hair. He often teased me saying he was going to cut my white hair and tie new fishing flies with it. I'd screech, giggle, and cover my hair with my hands.

Now my father's family was a different story all together. His mother, Elva, lived just outside of Boston. We visited Grammy Elva quite often, but Mom was very jealous of Dad's close relationship with her. Every time we left her house, she'd yell at

"Daddy's" face is obliterated for my protection.

him all the way home. "Lester, you bend over backwards to please your mother, but you won't get off your ass to do anything for me!"

Meanwhile, Dad had started a printing business in our basement. He worked for a printing company during the day and then worked the business at home in the evenings. He had several large presses, a big paper cutter, a light table, and some other equipment. The whole process fascinated me.

Our basement was huge and Dad's printing equipment took up less than half the cellar. On the other side, we had a ping-pong table near the washer and dryer. Mom and I sometimes played while she did the laundry.

One afternoon, Dad was in the cellar with us. He'd disappeared for a while, but we hadn't really paid any attention since we were preoccupied with our game of ping-pong. Finally, Dad gracefully glided around the foot of the stairs wearing Mom's wedding dress. Mom was about five feet eight inches tall and large busted so he fit into it pretty well. It was funny and as I was about to laugh when I heard, "Lester, take that off!" My mother's tone of voice and demeanor would have made anyone feel ashamed. I felt bad for Dad as my humor quickly turned to fear. I felt ashamed of myself for thinking it was funny and afraid my mother was going to be angry with me if she caught me smiling. Dad just turned and walked away without a word.

It had become perfectly normal for me to alter my own actions and hide my feelings to mitigate Mom's emotional explosions. Most of the time, I handled her outbursts by responding in total agreement and working to make her feel as if it was okay for her to act that way. This following incident was a little different though. It was the first time I recognized something was terribly wrong with my mother's mind and how much of a responsibility I had in taking care of her.

Mom told me our cat, Snowhite, had been run over by a car. We were sitting in her bedroom looking out the window and she was pointing down the road to where she'd supposedly been hit. A day or two had passed and she was still crying occasionally.

There was something white lying in the curve of the road and she was trying to convince me it was Snowhite. I humored her as I thought:

EVEN IF SNOWHITE WAS STILL ON THE ROAD, SHE WOULDN'T BE THAT WHITE ANYMORE… SHE'D BE ALL DIRTY AND MESSED UP… AND IF SHE IS STILL OUT THERE, WHY WOULD MOM LEAVE HER THERE?

Mom may have fabricated the whole scenario; she often did that. But this time, she frightened me with her blatant instability. I was getting old enough to see I was more logical than she was and I was only about five years old. There's no doubt she'd been like this for years, so I'd already assumed the role of **Caretaker** before I was old enough to consciously recognize the need.

Much later that year, Mom finally got her wish for a son. My baby brother was born late December 1966. My parents named him George.

I was simply fascinated when Mom brought him home. He was so tiny. She showed me how I could help her take care of him and I liked that. I was more than four years older than he was, so I didn't notice the brutal differences in the way she treated the two of us over the years, even in public. My family has made me aware of this over the years. I guess I just assumed it was because he was a little boy.

Obviously, Mom couldn't handle the normal ups and downs of life, so when the downs hit, she rarely handled it well. Now she was facing a life-threatening situation. Shortly after George was born, Mom was diagnosed with ovarian cancer. It was 1967 and medicine was not nearly as advanced as it is today, so it was a scary time. She was lucky and a hysterectomy stopped the cancer completely. Ironically, that scare wasn't what sent her into a deep depression. She was devastated because she couldn't have any more children. Then again, Aunt Jo had three children now.

Mom started drinking and running around a lot more. She often stayed out very late and Dad was angry. This is when I first remember him taking me to his room to play his version of the "game of love." I suspect he'd been **grooming** me for some time now.

I hated my little-girl body and wanted to be grown-up. So, I asked my mother, "When am I going to grow those?" referring to her breasts. She just told me I'd have them "soon enough."

My frustrations were very real and I waited for what seemed like forever for "them" to grow, but it just wasn't happening. I'd ask her again when "soon enough" was going to be. I was about to nag her for an answer once again, but I stopped myself. I was afraid she might get suspicious and wonder why I was so interested in having breasts. I didn't want her to know I needed them for Dad, so I never asked her again.

In the meantime, Mom was still grasping at ways to cure her seemingly incurable sadness. She was determined to fill the relentless emptiness she felt and her desperate need for feeling loved in any way she could. It took me years to understand why she wanted more children. I think she thought having children would fill an inner void that even she couldn't understand. I call it **'corrupted fulfillment.'**

Regardless of her motives, I was about six when we took in a foster child, Marie. I believe she was about 10 years old then. I think Mom got an older girl to babysit my brother and me so she could go drinking and run around with men more often.

Then we took in a foster boy, Willie. He was about my age. He had severe burn scars from just above his knees all the way up to his neck and down his arms to just above his elbows. Mom told me his pajamas caught on fire when he was trying to cook himself breakfast; his mother was in bed, drunk.

As my mother's running around and drinking increased, so did the fights. Mom needed an alibi if she was going to convince Dad she wasn't doing anything wrong while she was out at night. She decided to use me.

Ballet and tap dancing were one of my childhood passions. Mom always took me to my dancing classes, which were in the evenings. It worked out nicely for her because she could just drop me off and go to the bar while she "waited" for me. When class was over, all the parents picked up

their girls and I was often left standing in the doorway with no place to go.

My instructor simply took me back to the studio and continued to play the piano as if nothing was wrong. I danced harder than usual as I tried to avoid the feelings of embarrassment and abandonment. Minutes seemed like hours as I watched the hands slowly move on the big clock on the wall.

Anytime Mom felt guilty about something, like being late to pick me up, she was angry. She managed to make her bad mood everyone else's fault… in this case, mine. I was getting in the way of her lifestyle and she resented me for that.

It was the late 1960's and everything was different, from the lack of flame-retardant pajamas to the lack of laws that protected children. Mom figured that Dad wouldn't think she'd take me to the bars with her, so that's exactly what she did. Again, I was the perfect alibi.

There was a bar just down the road called the "Comet Club." The lady behind the bar always made me a sweet-tasting Shirley Temple. I got lots of attention there. People gave me quarters for the jukebox and I could sit at the bar, too. Now, there was another bar called "Mr. G's" where the Coca-Cola always tasted bitter and I had to sit in a dim corner by myself. I did like the bowling machine and the music though.

Unfortunately, Mom liked to go to Mr. G's, where the cola tasted bad. I'd sit in the corner by myself watching her flirt with all the men. She was embarrassing. She shoved her bust out, often in men's faces, or she'd lean on the bar so her bosoms were on display. Her strawberry, blonde hair was always curled beautifully and her makeup was flattering. She was very pretty, extremely flirty and the men flocked to her.

I'd think about Dad waiting at home. I felt sorry for him when songs like, "He'll Have to Go" by Jim Reeves played ("Put your sweet lips a little closer to the phone"). I imagined Dad making that phone call to Mom at the bar and asking her to leave the man she was drinking with. In my young mind, I thought if he did call her, it might make everything the way it used to be.

Little did I know; nothing was going to stop our lives from spiraling completely out of control.

4 - Willie and Marie

Mom was drinking more and harboring deeper, darker secrets. It's no wonder she was more abusive than ever. Even the fights between my parents were bordering on violence. Their screaming often woke me up in the middle of the night. I'd get out of bed and sit at the top of the stairs to listen. I always felt as if I was about to get in trouble, too.

I became angry and began acting out with violence. I suspect I was mimicking some of the abuse my mother inflicted on me. For instance, the slaps to the face she gave me when I was a toddler and learning to count. One day, I'd slapped my foster brother, Willie, across the face for some reason. His thick, Commonwealth-issued glasses fell to the floor. I was stunned to see his reaction; he just bent over, picked them up, and put them back on. Then he looked at me as if he expected me to do it again. I did because I didn't feel I'd made an impact on him the first time. He did the same thing again, waiting for another slap.

Then, as if this was some kind of circus act, I showed my oldest cousin, Craig, when we went on vacation in Maine. It fascinated me that anyone would simply let me do that to them.

I called Willie over and said to my cousin, "Watch this!" Willie knew what I was going to do and he stood in front of me, just like the last time, waiting. I hit him, his glasses fell to the ground, and he picked them up then stood there looking at me… waiting.

Much to my cousin's horror, I did it again. Craig was shocked I would do something so terrible. He scolded me harshly and drilled it into my head that I'd been horribly mean. Now, I felt ashamed, bad, and I didn't do it again. I always respected Craig as if he were my big brother. When he scolded me, it hurt my feelings and I listened.

Not long after, I got a glimpse into Willie's life and saw first-hand some of the things that happened to him that made him so "different." This series of events changed my entire outlook on him, and life in general.

Back home, Willie missed his own mother and asked if he could visit her. My mother reluctantly agreed and arranged to take him to see her.

I was kind of excited as we arrived at the apartment building. We walked up a flight of stairs toward his mother's apartment. My anticipation quickly turned to apprehension as I noticed the terrible condition of the building. Her apartment door had cracks and holes through it. Mom knocked and a faint voice behind the door told us to come in.

Mom and I stood in the kitchen doorway for a moment. My jaw dropped and we were both speechless as we looked upon the overwhelming filth. Piles of beer cans were strewn across the kitchen floor and the garbage can was overflowing. The sink was loaded with dirty dishes and the whole place smelled putrid.

It didn't faze Willie in the least; he bolted right past us and ran to his mother. Mom shook off the horror and was right on his heels.

I stood there in the doorway still stunned. There were no chairs at the kitchen table, which was covered in leftover foods, beer bottles, cans, and various other unidentifiable things.

While Mom and Willie were in his mother's bedroom, I started to snoop around a little. To the left of me was a doorway. I couldn't wait to see what surprise that room held, so I walked toward the door cautiously. I could see it was a bathroom, which was good since I had to use it anyway. I stepped into the room and stopped as my jaw dropped at the sight. The toilet was literally full. The raw waste was piled higher than the seat. The last person to take a crap must have stood over the toilet and just let it fall. There's no way they could have sat down.

I couldn't wait to get out of that place. I headed back into the kitchen as Mom barged through the doorway on the other side of the room and whatever she had seen, made her feel the same way. She was ranting and raving about Willie's mother and the way she was nearly passed out from booze and drugs. We left immediately.

It seemed like Mom yelled at Willie all the way home. She was angry and obviously couldn't understand why he was so happy to see his mother. There's no doubt in my mind she also felt slighted thinking she was a blessing to him compared to his own mother. As the sound of my mother's nagging voice became background noise, I thought hard about Willie; I wanted to understand why he felt so compelled to be with his mother. What I was able to realize is that, good or bad, she was all he'd ever known; she was all he ever had until he came to live with us. That's when I began to feel sorry for him and I understood more about how he became such a mess.

As Mom's tolerance for any kind of disruption—including her children—continued to dwindle, and her angry outbursts became more frequent, we all walked around on eggshells. Even Dad was in self-preservation mode and kept out of her way most of the time.

At dinner, Willie always sat at the table with his head down. His face was practically parallel with his plate. Mom constantly told him to keep his head up, but it was only a matter of minutes before he was staring into his plate again. Mom had enough one night and hit him on the top of his head with the dull side of a 10-inch slicing knife she always kept by her plate. Everyone at the table tensed up. I cringed and dropped my own head thinking how senseless it was to hit him:

THAT ISN'T GOING TO MAKE HIM HOLD HIS HEAD UP.

No one said a word to my mother when she went off like this since that would only make her angrier. I understand she had her hands full with Willie and his bag of problems, but she was about to go overboard.

Willie often urinated and defecated in his pants. Each time he did it, Mom spanked him. She became extremely frustrated because he just wouldn't stop. After all, he was six years old.

Well, he'd done it again and I heard Mom downstairs spanking him with a brush. I just expected him to be bawling because she'd been spanking him way too long. With every second that passed, I expected her to stop, but she didn't. I wanted to stop her so badly I was twitching. I was as afraid for myself as I was for him, so I just waited, barely breathing. Finally, she stopped and I took a deep breath. He wasn't crying; he never did.

Willie came upstairs and quietly went to his room across the hall. I made sure Mom was nowhere around and then went to his room. I was horrified to see what she'd done to him; I ordered him to show me his fanny. He pulled down the back of his pajamas and I almost cried. Willie's entire little butt was purple and blue and it was turning black in places. It still hurts me to think about it. I hugged him and tried to make him feel better; maybe I needed consoling, too. Then, I had a motherly talk with him hoping to make him understand that he really had to stop messing in his pants.

I think Willie's beating injured me more than it did him. I couldn't bear to watch it happen again, but she wasn't going to do it again either. What she was about to do was almost more disturbing than the beating.

Mom told me privately that she "couldn't" spank Willie anymore. I was stunned and relieved at the same time. I asked her why. She said, "I asked him point-blank: Do you like Mamma to spank you?" Much to her surprise (and mine), he answered, "Yes."

THAT EXPLAINS... WHY HE LET ME HIT HIM... OH NO... I'M TERRIBLE! OH THAT POOR KID! I FEEL AWFUL.

She continued, telling me she'd noticed his penis was hard after spanking him. Of course, I'm overly sensitive to the subject and my young mind began to wonder why she told me about it in the first place. I didn't know how I was "supposed" to respond. I was afraid to let it show that I knew she was talking about something sexual, so I dropped my head and didn't say anything.

Now, Mom needed another form of punishment for Willie. So, she decided to make him stand in the corner of the small room in the center of the house, which led to the kitchen, bathroom, living room, and dining room, with his soiled underpants on his head. It was impossible not to walk past him frequently. Mom wanted Marie and me to laugh at him. I didn't think it was funny anymore. Actually, there wasn't much that was funny about Willie anymore. I was afraid *not* to show some kind of amusement since that's what my mother wanted and to save my own ass. After a few times I just couldn't do it to him anymore, so I made myself scarce when she humiliated him.

In the midst of our chaos, my parents built a social life, mostly of my mother's doing. So it wasn't any coincidence when they got friendly with a married couple who lived near Mr. G's. You guessed it; Mom was having an affair with the husband. I remember him and his wife coming to our house to party with Mom and Dad on several occasions. They rode motorcycles and Mom loved to ride although Dad didn't seem to care for it very much. I kept telling Mom and Dad how much I wanted to learn how to ride so they finally got me a minibike for my seventh birthday. Mom's boyfriend taught me how to ride.

Mom was also seeing another man, Tim. I'd seen him a few times in the bars and at his apartment with Mom. She was with him the first time I saw her have sex right in front of me. Sometimes she'd do it in the front seat of a car while I sat in the back waiting.

Anyway, she said she knew Dad was giving me the third degree about what she did while we were out at night. So now, Mom and I also had our little secrets Dad could never know.

It's no surprise Dad was becoming more inquisitive and more clever with his third degrees. One night while I watched him work the printing presses in the basement, he started talking with me about Mom's affair as if it was old news. He told me she'd already told him all about her new boyfriend. I was young, but it did cross my mind he might have been trying to trick me, so I tried to keep my guard up. Anyway, he kept talking about him as if he knew the guy and I became quite engrossed in the one-sided conversation. Then right in the middle of his sentence, he stopped as if he were trying to remember Tim's name and asked, "Hohm.... darn, what's his name again?"

I just wanted him to finish his story and I said, "Tim."

As soon as his name passed my lips, I knew I'd screwed up. I don't remember any more of his questions. All I could do was begin worrying about what Mom was going to do to me when she got home and with good reason.

As soon as she found out, she started screaming at me. I stood in front of her trembling in fear as she violently yelled at me. Out of all her yelling and screaming, these are the only words I remember: "He tricked you, and you should have known better!"

I was angry with myself for being stupid and angrier with her for making me lie in the first place. She was the one being bad and I was paying the price from both of them.

At some point over the past year, I started having strange, overwhelming feelings of nausea, helplessness, and paralyzing fear. Mom said I turned pale each time one of these episodes came on. It happened sporadically, but quickly, and there was no one feeling or symptom I could accurately describe. But each time it happened, I cried for my mother. Now, I'd never "needed" my mother this way and I felt like a baby. Actually, I regressed to an infantile state during these episodes.

Mom finally took me to the doctor since these "spells," as she called them, wouldn't stop, and became more frequent. Our doctor couldn't figure it out, so she took me to another one. The doctors didn't know what was wrong, so the spells continued undiagnosed.

The hardest part of having the spells was the way Marie teased me about them. She called me a baby and mimicked me when I cried.

Marie and I weren't very close, but we did do some typical, sister-like things. We often talked and giggled in bed for a little while after the lights went out. Dad usually yelled at us to shut up. We tried to quiet down, but one of us usually broke the silence and Dad would yell again. We'd either shut-up or he'd simply called me to the foot of the stairs where I got a belt whipping that left thick welts on my thighs and butt, then he'd take me to his bedroom. Some nights, he'd just skip the whipping. I remember feeling afraid that Marie might figure out what was going on.

After a while, the belt whippings became less frequent, but the trips to Dad's room came more often and I wanted to get out of it.

I WONDER WHAT HE'LL DO IF WE DON'T TALK AT ALL?

So, I decided to try an experiment. That night, I didn't say a word just to see what he'd do. Marie started chatting, but I pretended I'd fallen asleep. The silence fell and I laid there waiting for… whatever.

Then, I heard his footsteps coming. He stopped at the foot of the stairs. Other than the pounding of my heart, there was complete silence. I didn't even breathe as the moment lingered and the sound of quiet screamed in my ears. I knew he was standing there listening and I was hoping he'd just go away when he bellowed, "Be quiet!"

A jolt of fear went through my body. I knew then he was sick; we hadn't made a peep. I felt numb as he walked away. Marie made a comment about how foolish he was, but I was so stunned I didn't say anything. I laid there trying to figure out why he did it, but it only made me more afraid.

Within what seemed like only a few minutes, I heard him coming again. He stopped at the foot of the stairs, but this time, he just called me to his room. Like a trained animal, I didn't even think, I just got up and went downstairs to his room.

When I got there, he took his clothes off and then he undressed me. He put me on the bed and he laid down. I was kneeling beside him waiting for instructions. He told me to suck it. I didn't like the looks of the "wet stuff" on the end of his penis; I thought it was pee. My face scrunched all up as if to say, "ewwwww" and I pointed to it and asked, "What's this wet stuff?"

He said, "It's just pre-come; it tastes like sugar and water."

I figured this was another one of his lies just to get me to do it. It was gross, but I didn't think I had a choice. I quickly licked it as if it were going to bite me and thought:

*It isn't that bad...*and I proceeded as if nothing was wrong.

Then, all of a sudden, he made me stop. He was so abrupt that he scared me; I thought I'd done something wrong. I watched him closely as he sat up, got off the bed, and quickly walked to the foot of the bed. Then, he grabbed me by the legs and pulled me across the silky bedspread. He wasn't gentle, so now I was really frightened. My rear-end was right at the edge of the bed. Then he put his hand down on me and said, "Jesus, you're already wet!"

He seemed happy with that, but I felt guilty and confused.

IS THAT GOOD OR BAD? IS HE MAD AT ME?

I watched his face as he knelt on the floor at the foot of the bed. He looked strange, but now, at least I knew he wasn't angry with me. He put his penis up against me and pushed, but it hurt, so I pulled back a little, which caused him to slip beneath me. Still, he began sliding it back and forth and I just laid there watching his face as he moved.

HE LOOKS FUNNY... AND HE SOUNDS FUNNY, TOO.

He started moaning and said, "I got it in you, I got it in you!"

Somehow, I knew what he was supposed to have done. All I could do was watch his funny-looking expression and think how hysterical it was that he didn't even know it wasn't in me. I didn't dare laugh because I was afraid he'd get mad, but the urge was building and I couldn't keep it in any longer. I turned my head to the side and pretended to cough, to hide my laughter.

Finally, he stopped. When he pulled away, I scurried away from him. Then, he looked down at the bed, saw the wetness, and realized what he'd done. His mood quickly shifted, his face grimaced, and he sharply said, "Why didn't you say something? I wasn't even in you!"

He kept looking at me and really expected me to answer. Now I was afraid again and my feelings were hurt because it was obvious he was angry. He seemed so disgusted. I just dropped my head and answered, "I don't know."

I'm not sure when Dad came to the foot of the stairs again, but when he did, he called Marie to his room. Like I had in the past, she got up in the similar programmed, robotic fashion and went to his room without saying a word.

As bizarre as it may sound, I felt devastated. I was crushed. I thought Dad didn't love me anymore because I'd disappointed him so badly. I was angry with myself for not doing what he'd wanted the right way. Now he didn't want me anymore. I was convinced he'd called Marie to his room because she was older. Her body was maturing and mine was still a little girl's body, the one I loathed so much.

In a moment of anger and utter confusion, I took a red pen and colored my nipples and my pubic area with big, dark, red dots. My thinking, at the time, was that Dad would like it, but after I'd done it, I realized that it didn't wash off.

I figured that Mom would be furious with me when she noticed the horrible blotches on me. I tried to hide them, but they stood out like a clown's nose on my pale, white skin.

Initially, she seemed shocked at the sight of my artwork. Then, she asked me why I'd done it. I felt thoroughly embarrassed and I knew I couldn't tell her why. I just dropped my head and answered with my typical, "I don't know." Contrary to her usual incessant demands for answers, she dropped the subject as if she didn't want to know.

As I look back, I didn't know I'd shoved all of my own problems aside—putting them into some kind of insignificant pile. In comparison to the severity of the abuse Willie had faced at the hands of my mother and his own, the abuse in my own life seemed trivial. Even the sexual abuse Marie was suffering from Dad was a mere form of competition. There's no doubt I had **minimized my own abuse** and began to avoid my problems by consuming myself with Willie's.

After Dad's failed attempt to have intercourse with me, I don't think he called me to his room again. I have no doubt Marie was not only more compliant, but also more capable of handling whatever he wanted from her. As time passed without Dad abusing me, the memories became buried, blocked-out, and forgotten. The spells even stopped, but unfortunately, my reprieve was only temporary.

5 - Feeling Memories

For as long as I can remember, I had nightmares of being chased through abandoned buildings in old western towns with no way out. I'd often wake up in the middle of the night with my heart pounding so hard in my chest. I could feel the vibration in my face and head. I never saw what was after me, but I was petrified. At least now, I was able to get through the nights uninterrupted by Dad's sexual desires.

Unfortunately, he was getting everything he wanted from Marie including an ally in his continuing investigation into Mom's affairs. Marie was about 12 years old now. It wouldn't have been difficult for Dad to give her just what she needed to feel as if she had more value; something none of us felt much. We were all starving for attention, recognition, or anything that would make us feel a little self-worth—even if it was painful. Willie was a perfect example.

I was off the hook in another way, too; I wasn't getting the third degree from Dad anymore. Marie had spilled the beans this time and told Dad the name of Mom's favorite bar. He got the phone number to Mr. G's and called her there.

This is not how I'd imagined this phone call would go and I guarantee you that "Put Your Sweet Lips a Little Closer to the Phone" was not playing.

I'd been in my room and heard Dad yelling. I didn't know what was happening. I came downstairs to the kitchen and Marie told me what had happened. I sat down to listen. I wondered what the people in the bar were thinking since I could hear Mom screaming through the phone from across the room.

When she was through yelling at Dad, she apparently asked to speak to Marie since he handed the phone to her. She said "Hello," and then didn't say another word. Mom wasn't screaming anymore and the quiet murmur of her voice sent a shiver down my spine. Marie continued to listen in silence and then hung up. Without a word, she went to our room. I quickly followed behind trying to find out what Mom had said. Marie silently began packing; Mom had kicked her out.

I started crying and Dad begged her to stay. I tried to convince her that Mom didn't mean it, but she seemed determined to go. Then I watched the way Dad talked to her and, for just a moment, I could see something much deeper between them that I'd forgotten about. I turned and left the room feeling a bit resentful and partly not caring anymore if she stayed or went. Then, I chose to forget the ugly memory again.

Regardless, Dad convinced Marie to stay and I never heard anyone mention it again. As far as I know, they swept it all under the rug like so many other events in our lives.

From my own experiences with Mom, I'm sure Marie paid dearly for telling on her in ways I never saw and in others that I've chosen to forget. My mother is ruthless and unforgiving.

A lot had changed, again, and in a short time. My parents' marriage was now ready to split and I knew it. Friends and family didn't come around anymore. I wasn't even welcomed at the neighbor's house in quite the same way. We gradually stopped going to church, too.

Mom was still searching for happiness somewhere "out there" and Dad was trying to figure out how to keep his wife at home. I just tried to get through each day without sparking my mother's fragile and unpredictable temper. It became easier for her to slap me in the face for little to no reason, often just to blow off steam.

I rarely looked her in the eyes; she terrified me. I can still hear her belittling and condescending tone of voice. I tried, but I rarely measured up to her standards. I just kept trying harder anyway. I gradually and unknowingly geared my whole life's purpose toward making Mom proud of me, to approve of me, to acknowledge something good in me. I needed a sense that she loved me, but instead, I felt as if I were a stupid, unworthy, hopeless failure.

I often think Mom either knew, or at least suspected, that Dad had been molesting Marie and me. I also think she resented us deeply for it, which may have been another reason she treated us so badly. She never treated my little brother with the same hatred. Never.

Because of my strained relationship with Marie, the deep sorrow I had for Willie and nearly five years difference between my brother and me, I isolated myself from everyone. Thankfully, I had some four-legged help.

I don't remember when we got him, but we had a dog we'd named Charlie Brown. He was a wonderful pet and, at this time in my life, he was my best friend. I got to a point where I felt safest when I was spending time alone with him in the woods. He was a good-size dog at about sixty-five pounds. I often hugged him and cried. He seemed to listen, or at least I thought he did.

I certainly couldn't cry in front of Mom. If I showed any sign of feeling upset or if she thought I was about to cry, she'd get more angry. I know it's a common cliché, but when she said, "Shut up or I'll give you something to cry about," she meant she'd make me feel worse for crying. Eventually, I learned to hide my emotions almost completely. No matter what Mom did to me, whether it was physical or emotional, I no longer cried in front of her. In a way, it was good because this was like boot camp of sorts preparing me for the hell I could never have imagined was still to come.

Then one day, she sat me down to talk. I didn't know whether to be afraid or not. I'd never heard her voice sound so serious yet so gentle. Then she asked, "How would you like it if we lived in Maine?"

At the age of eight, I'm sure I didn't understand what the impact of moving to Grand Lake Stream would have on my family or me. I felt a little excited remembering our vacations there. The entire family seemed happier then and Mom and Dad didn't fight. She was always nagging at him at home; "Lester do this, Lester do that," and she constantly berated him. Whatever he did was never quite right or good enough. I don't know how he put up with it.

Anyway, she waited for my response and I could sense that she expected me to have an answer right then. I also thought she was looking for a certain answer. I looked up at her to help figure out what she wanted.

With a bit of apprehension, I nervously said I'd like to live in Maine hoping I was "right." I was instantly relieved to see she approved.

Regardless, my parents didn't seem to waste any time preparing to move. They sold the printing business and all the equipment. I remember hearing heated discussions between them about not getting what it was worth, but that was just the first beating our family would take in this major undertaking.

It isn't unusual for people and families with problems to search out a cure for their deteriorating lives. It also isn't unusual that, like us, they waste precious time and energy looking for answers in all the wrong places. It's called the "geographical cure." It's when a family or person thinks that moving away will leave the problems behind. It's about as effective as trying to move away from the flu—we will take it with us.

Regardless, we moved to Maine in 1971. It was the summer I turned nine. Coincidentally, my parents bought our house from Aunt Jo and Uncle Tony. They had just moved to Grand Lake a few years earlier and bought a bigger house down the street.

Our house was the last one on a dead-end street at the edge of the lake. You couldn't beat the location, but it was a far cry from our home in Massachusetts. The house was probably nearing 100 years old at the time.

There are still only seven paved streets in town and each one dead end except the one coming into town and a dirt road heading into miles of vast wilderness.

The major industry is logging for a paper mill. A huge portion of the trees came from the forests around Grand Lake Stream.

Our next-door neighbors were a sweet, older couple. They had a very attractive daughter in her early twenties who lived at home. She'd be the cause of many fights to come.

Meanwhile, Dad had landed a job working for the local newspaper in Calais about 30 miles away. I got the distinct impression he wasn't happy there; he didn't seem happy at all anymore. I'm sure this was a huge change for him. After all, he was a city boy.

Both my parents were changing. They seemed distant and I hardly knew what to expect from them anymore. Mom had become unappreciative of everything. Even when someone tried to do something nice, she'd find fault with it. She never ceased to amaze me with her ability to make a person feel such dread when the whole intent was to create joy.

This time, she disgusted me with an undeserved, brutal tongue-lashing. I couldn't even muster up anything to help substantiate her rotten attitude the way I usually did.

We had a choice of three, family-owned cabins on different lakes in the area, which we could use. Mom decided we were going to the cabin on Wabash Lake for a few days. We had to drive about 10 miles of dirt road to get to the lake, load all the supplies onto a boat, then go down the lake to the cabin. The boat was an aluminum skiff and the motor was failing. Mom kept nursing it along, or maybe it was more like 'cursing' it along, so it would run.

Dad was working in Calais and traveled all the way out to Wabash afterward. He drove as far as the lakeshore and we picked him up about the same time each night.

This time, he was late. As we waited, I walked around in the woods and enjoyed myself while my mother and brother waited together. Mom was getting noticeably irritated as the time passed. She'd probably finished her drink and didn't bring another one.

I'm not sure how late he was, but Dad finally pulled into sight. I noticed he had a self-satisfied grin on his face, which Mom quickly wiped clean with a blast of angry scolding. "Where the hell have you been, Lester?" She continued screaming at him for keeping her waiting. He couldn't get one word out because she wouldn't stop yelling. She finally stopped—probably only to breathe—and he began to explain.

He said he'd bought something for her and he headed for the trunk. Mom actually stayed quiet. I felt embarrassed for her when he opened the trunk and showed her a brand new motor for the boat. I smiled and looked at Mom waiting for her reaction, but much to my surprise, she just continued to criticize his tardiness instead of thanking him. "You made me wait and worry Lester."

WORRIED? WHAT A CROCK! YOU WERE JUST PISSED BECAUSE HE MADE YOU WAIT... PERIOD.

She didn't worry much about anything anymore unless it was about herself. Finally, I got angry because she wouldn't stop berating him. This is when I'd normally try to substantiate her idiocy, but I just couldn't do it and I yelled, "Mom!" in a sharp tone of voice.

I frightened myself because I'd never spoken to her that way. I waited for her to explode at me for being disrespectful, but much to my surprise, she calmed down immediately.

They hooked the new motor on the boat. Then, to add insult to injury, she found fault with it. She said in a sour tone, "The rip cord pulls too hard. It isn't any better than the old one."

I felt sick. We'd become a miserable bunch.

I always enjoyed the forest behind the house in Massachusetts, so it was easy for me to fall in love with the wilderness here. I explored the woods and dirt roads with wide-eyed wonder. It wasn't unusual at all to see a bear, moose, or deer since the wildlife was abundant; and still is.

Fortunately, we'd brought my mini-bike. I started doing stunts and could do an airborne jump so well Mom nicknamed me "Evil Knievel."

It seemed hard for me to make friends being so new in town. I submerged myself in riding and exploring the old dirt roads and forests that summer. It was an easy way for me to avoid people.

Fall had come and the school year was beginning. I thought it might be fun since I'd always enjoyed it before.

I started fourth grade and they were teaching a lot of the same material I'd already learned the year before. Sometimes I felt disappointed and other times, I thought it was neat because I already knew the answers to the teacher's questions.

At first, I started making friends. I played jacks during recess with some of the girls. My new teacher was a different story. She seemed easily agitated and didn't like me for some reason. This made my adjustment period more difficult. I remember taking an assignment up to her desk. I waited nervously as she looked at it. Then she yelled, "What the hell is this mess?"

I was stunned. No teacher ever talked to me that way and I couldn't imagine what I'd done wrong. She didn't make it clear as to what the "mess" was; she just didn't like it.

The teacher finally called Mom in for a conference. Mom didn't tolerate me misbehaving in any way, so I was scared. Surprisingly, my teacher only baffled Mom with her petty complaints. She criticized my accent and said I was "different." As the conference was winding down, my teacher asked Mom if she used a brush on me for spanking purposes. Mom said, yes. Then, my teacher said, "Next time, try the bristles."

After the meeting, Mom talked to some other parents who weren't surprised by what she'd said and done. Apparently, this teacher had a reputation for being mean. So thankfully, my mother disregarded it, but it didn't make it any easier for me in the classroom.

I still don't know what sparked her dislike for me and I don't remember doing anything bad. Nonetheless, I'd irritated her so much that she shoved my desk and me to the back wall of the classroom. I felt like such an idiot sitting in the back of the class all by myself. And, of course, the kids took advantage of my conspicuous isolation and teased me terribly.

It wasn't surprising to me when my teacher's daughter ran away from home later that year. There were posters of her plastered all over town. I closely examined one of them. Her dark hair framed her pretty face making her eyes stand out. I tried to read into her eyes as if she could tell me something from the poor photocopy. The picture made me sad.

Anyway, this is probably when my socializing skills deteriorated even more. I hadn't learned to stand up for myself. I didn't know how to handle it when the kids picked on me or simply teased me. I just felt hurt, shut my mouth, and retreated into myself.

That non-defensive behavior came from my "training" at home. I'd learned to clam-up whenever Mom scolded or ridiculed me. If I said anything in my own defense, it only made her furious.

Now it was late fall and deer hunting season had started. It was a yearly major event since deer meat was a staple to many families. Almost everyone hunted, including some girls and many of the women. Dad openly showed his lack of interest and Mom didn't like it. I could tell he didn't want to go hunting at all. Mom insisted with her usual disgusted and degrading demand, "You *will* go. You're not going to embarrass me by sitting home on your ass while the rest of us go hunting." Of course—once again—it was all about her. She didn't just insist he go hunting, but that he also act as if he enjoyed it.

Winter came quickly bringing tons of snow. It sometimes stayed at sub-zero temperatures for weeks. The wind blowing off the lake often made the wind-chill temperatures dip to fifty below zero. Still, I enjoyed the outdoors and all the activities; even in the wintertime; especially riding snowmobiles through the trails in the woods. Mom often packed enough supplies for a weekend and we'd head off into the woods to one of the cabins. During the day, we ice fished and rode the snowmobiles through the trails and on the lakes. At night, we stayed inside by the fire trying to thaw out from the day.

Life was certainly different in Maine than it was in the suburbs of Massachusetts. I'd learned some interesting things that were basic to the way of life here. Mom did show me how to shoot a rifle and pistol. Most of the time, she wouldn't take the time to teach me anything. There were a lot more things I didn't know. I remember asking how to do a lot of things over the years and she'd avoid me. Of course, I didn't nag since that would make her angry. I didn't learn how to cook, hunt properly, or do much of anything—unless it was the chores she didn't want to do—like cleaning fish, for instance.

Meanwhile, my parents' attempt at a geographical cure was a complete failure. They argued over little things that didn't matter in the least. As I've said before, if you weren't interested in what Mom wanted or liked, you were wrong or weird. She even ridiculed Dad for eating his eggs over easy because she didn't like them that way. She'd treated me that way from such a young age so I even pretended her favorite color was also mine.

To make matters worse, Dad and his boss weren't getting along. Of course, Mom told Dad he was wrong. I knew Dad had a good business in Massachusetts and he seemed to know the printing business very well. Regardless, he soon lost his job at the newspaper.

Dad was entrepreneurial by nature and bought a propane gas business. The following spring, he had a huge wooden platform built in the back yard to store the one-hundred-pound tanks. He bought a big, flatbed truck to carry the gas tanks and deliver them to homes and camps. Most people had gas stoves in their homes and all the camps used propane for light and refrigeration.

The new business wasn't making much money, so Mom got a job at the paper mill. She started working three rotating shifts: seven to three, three to 11, and 11 to seven. This is when my life took a drastic turn for the worse. Nothing I'd experienced up to now prepared me for any of this.

It was a warm spring day and the sun was shining down from a clear blue sky with only a few, bright, white puffy clouds. Hundreds of flowers and trees were blooming and the sounds of birds filled the air. My cousin, Frankie, and I were playing on his front lawn.

We got into a silly argument. I'm sure I said something nasty to him because he retaliated by yelling, "Your father isn't your father anyway!"

It hit me so hard and I stood there paralyzed, mind and body. I didn't know whether to believe him or not. "He is... so." I said, but something inside me caved in. I didn't know what it was, but it didn't feel good.

I turned and ran home feeling a hollow ache in my chest. I took a moment to think before I got too upset and decided to ask Mom if it was true.

She was in the kitchen when I got home. I told her what Frankie had said. She didn't look at me and didn't say anything either. She immediately went to the telephone on the wall and made a call. I remember feeling very irritated because she'd completely ignored me, but I wouldn't have dared to say a word.

Then, she started yelling into the phone. It was obvious she had called Aunt Jo. I don't remember what Mom said, but she was verbally brutal.

I knew then Frankie must have been telling the truth or she wouldn't have gone off like that. I wanted answers, but I had to wait for her to finish her telephone tantrum. She'd become so vicious, I felt sorry for my aunt. I sat waiting impatiently as she screamed with hardly a pause and I started to think.

A bundle of confused feelings began to emerge about the only father I ever knew. I was upset because Mom had lied to me in the first place and I wondered why. Oddly, I didn't feel like crying because it didn't hurt. The feelings it stirred within me disturbed me more than anything did.

As I sat there thinking and analyzing my own confusion, I started to remember something Dad used to do, but I couldn't quite put my finger on it. It was more of a "feeling memory" than a visual or verbal memory. I just felt very uneasy about whatever "it" was.

I became extremely consumed by my inner turmoil. Then I realized I had to shake it off so I could pay attention when my mother finally hung up the phone. Then she sat down with me and reluctantly explained the story:

"Your father's name is Alan Waters. He left us when you were about two years old. He drank a lot, didn't work much and I supported the three of us most of the time. He didn't take very good care of you while I was working. I'd often come home to find him passed out drunk and you'd be running around without a diaper. Anyway, later on, I met Lester and married him. Daddy loves you very much and he even adopted you so you would have his name."

When she told me, "Daddy loves you very much," the first thing that came to mind without any conscious effort was:

IF YOU ONLY KNEW HOW MUCH.

I couldn't completely understand my thoughts and feelings at the time. I suspect my subconscious knew, but my conscious mind was unable to admit that he'd done such things to me.

Then, a sickening "feeling memory." overwhelmed me. No visuals or anything like that, just a gut feeling. Apparently, I'd blocked out all the sexual abuse and didn't know how to deal with Dad now. I didn't dare ask any questions either. I needed time to absorb everything Mom had told me and to try to deal with all the horrible feelings and obscure memories.

My mother gave me no consoling, no long chat, just the explanation, end of story. I don't think she cared how I felt and if she did, she didn't show it. I went outside and paced around the yard thinking. I wondered why my father would leave me and never call or want to see me again. Now, I was hurt.

On the other hand, I also felt a strange sense of relief to find out that Dad wasn't my real father. It may have been the reason I began to remember. Deep down, I knew what he'd done to me when I was younger—sick, perverted things—but he was far from finished.

6 - "We're Sisters"

It was well into the middle of the night. I was sound asleep when something tickled my leg. I was still half-asleep and tried brushing it away, but it didn't stop. Whatever it was woke me up. I was horrified when I realized it was Dad, or Lester, my stepfather. It didn't matter; he was under the blankets, crawling up onto the end of my bed. I begged him to stop and tried to push him away, but he kept coming. I didn't know what to do. I just kept saying, "No Dad!—Don't.—Please!" as he got on top of me.

I was only 10 years old and he easily overpowered me. I don't remember feeling anything as he raped me. I just turned my head to one side and pretended it wasn't happening.

When he was done, he simply left the room. I don't know when I eventually gathered all my senses. It wasn't long before I started to remember when he'd tried the same thing when I was little. All those buried memories were beginning to return in bits and pieces.

I knew this wouldn't be the last time; and it wasn't. He came into my room and raped me many times after that. One time I heard him say, "Look what you make Daddy do." It didn't take much for me to blame myself; everything was always my fault. Understanding why he'd do it to begin with was impossible for me.

It was easy for him now since Mom was working all those weird shifts. At least she had a legitimate reason for being out all night.

I was afraid to tell anyone what he'd done, especially my mother since I thought she'd blame me. Knowing how vicious she could be, I didn't know what she'd do to me. Even more pitifully, although she had become somewhat removed, she was my only companion now. I was afraid of losing that and being completely alone. I thought she'd hate me.

Many of those feeling memories started to become vivid, visual memories. Now I was angry. I felt stupid because I'd been walking around all this time oblivious to the past events. I'd buried the horrible memories.

HE PROBABLY DOESN'T KNOW I'D FORGOTTEN EVERYTHING HE USED TO DO. I'LL BET HE THINKS I DIDN'T MIND WHAT HE'D DONE TO ME BECAUSE I NEVER ACTED LIKE ANYTHING HAPPENED BECAUSE I COULDN'T REMEMBER!

My scattered thoughts and attempts to rationalize what he was doing to me only made me furious. I wanted to say something, get angry with him, show my anger, or do something. I was too afraid to talk about it, even to him. I just shoved all my feelings deep inside and kept my mouth shut.

It wasn't long before those dreaded "spells" I used to have when I was little returned. Several decades had passed before I made a correlation between the "spells" and the abuse. Regardless, at the time, Mom decided to take me to the doctor again. She immediately told him about the head injury from falling down the stairs at 16 months old. The doctor said the spells were "probably" epileptic seizures caused by that injury.

Without any further testing, he prescribed two powerful barbiturates: Phenobarbital and Dilantin. The drugs didn't stop the spells, but Mom was insistent I take them faithfully. Of course, they kept me quite sedated, which I think she quickly learned to like. I was already easy to control, now I was under the influence of barbiturates, which made me as easily controlled as warm putty in her hand.

Some of my mother's discontent with her marriage may have been because Dad didn't show her much affection. I'm sure he lost interest after finding out about her many affairs, or maybe he simply preferred children.

Well, my mother had a trick up her sleeve that was going to loosen Dad up a little. She had a bag of marijuana and decided to put it in spaghetti sauce she was making for dinner. Then, she spiced up Dad's plate with a conspicuous amount. "What's all this green stuff?" he asked. She casually told him it was oregano and he started to eat.

I kept watching him as if something were going to happen right away. About the time I started to get bored from waiting, Mom went into the living room and sat in his lap while he was reading the newspaper. He laughed, played, and joked with her. He usually didn't like to be disturbed while he was reading his paper. They were very nice for a while that day. I can't remember feeling much of anything from what she put in the sauce, but she didn't put any "extra" on my plate either.

When there wasn't anyone in town to party with, Mom went to the bars in Calais. I know because she started taking me with her. One bar was the local biker's hangout. Of course, Mom drank heavily, so she was always drunk by the time we left.

Calais is a little more than 30 miles from home, so it was a considerable drive for any intoxicated person. One night after she turned the corner onto the 10-mile stretch of the Grand Lake road, she pulled the car to the side of the road and stopped. She looked at me and I was already looking at her wondering why she stopped. "You drive," she blurted out. I was 10.

I was in shock but didn't say a word. She turned the inside lights on, pushed the brake pedal, pointed at it and said, "This is the brake." Then, pointing to the gas pedal with her foot she said, "This is the gas." Then she wiggled the steering wheel and said, "You just steer it. Put the shift lever into 'D' for Drive and go. You can do it."

I said, "Okay." Like a good little girl, I got out of the car and walked around to the driver side while she slid over to the passenger side. I put the car in "D for drive" and slowly pulled away.

I was nervous as I waited for her to tell me I was doing something wrong. When a minute or two had passed and she hadn't criticized me, I looked over at her wondering why. She had passed out. I was glad since she couldn't yell at me.

I drove home a lot after that. Mom often referred to me as her "sidekick" to her friends. I liked it because I thought she liked having me around. I later learned that wasn't the case at all. Regardless, anytime she said, "Let's go," I went without question or hesitation.

Then, she told me not to call her "Mom" while we were in the bar. "We're sisters," she said with a big, encouraging, but devilish smile. She'd get angry if I'd slip and call her Mom and the dirty looks she gave me always scared the hell out of me. I quickly learned to keep her on a first name basis while we were out.

Mom was only 29 and didn't hide the fact that she dreaded the "big 3-0." I'm sure part of her strategy with the "sisters" thing was to make herself appear younger. There was more to it though. Our charade also made me appear older. That wasn't hard to do since I was already developing into a young woman, physically anyway.

Meanwhile, a lot of bitterness was developing between Mom and Aunt Jo. My mother's jealousy and resentment toward her became more obvious as our situation at home got worse. Her reputation as a drunk and a floozy had quickly spread through our small community and was affecting the whole family.

During our first year in Maine, we'd done a lot with my grandparents and my aunt and uncle. We weren't spending much time with family at all anymore. My aunt told my mother she was hurting everyone around her. The family said they felt sorry for Lester since Dad appeared to be the victim. That really irritated me, but I said nothing.

At the time, I didn't realize how afraid I'd become of Mom's violent temper. As I've said before, fear was just a normal feeling for me and it controlled my every thought and decision. I didn't do anything anymore without considering my mother's potential reaction. She frequently used me as a whipping boy to vent her anger. I didn't have to do anything wrong, so I never knew when to expect the next battering.

When I made the simplest mistake, Mom slapped me across my face. It wasn't much different from when I was learning to count. One of the things I had trouble with was telling time, especially when it was between 20 after and 20 before the hour. I'd made the mistake of getting the hour wrong a couple of times and she slapped me silly. I probably made her late for something. I was petrified every time she asked me for the time. She rarely taught me the right way to do anything; she'd just tell me I was stupid.

I wasn't the only one getting the brunt of her violence. My parents' arguments usually started inside the house and, as the arguing escalated to fighting, they'd go outside into the yard where they screamed and yelled at each other wildly. It was an embarrassing public display of violence.

Obviously, Dad was hurt and angry with her running around. He tried to keep her at home with no success. This time, he decided to take a distributor wire off her car so she couldn't start it. It didn't take her long to figure out what the problem was and she blew a gasket. She scared me more than ever before as I watched her anger grow more intense by the second.

When she was angry, the look in her eyes could scare the paint off the walls. I glanced at her as the scowl on her face distorted every pretty feature she had. She ordered me into the passenger seat of Dad's propane delivery truck. Of course, I got in without hesitation. I knew we weren't going for a joy ride. She started the truck and headed down the driveway. She drove toward the lake. I was horrified as she picked up speed and drove right into the lake. The truck stopped, she opened the door and water flooded in. She seemed satisfied.

My mother didn't care how embarrassing or humiliating her demands were; I'm not sure she knew how ridiculous she sounded either. She expected me to do whatever she wanted, no matter how ludicrous.

She was preparing to go out again and she intended to get one step ahead of Dad this time. She handed me her favorite long slicing knife—the same one she whacked Willie with—and told me to go out to the car and sit on the hood with it. I couldn't believe it. I knew I wouldn't really use the knife to hurt anyone. I also knew how ridiculous I looked. How I felt didn't matter and I'd better do it whether I liked it or not since the consequences would be much more painful than the humiliation.

I felt asinine in front of the neighbors, but it was safer to make an ass out of myself than to say, "No," to Mom. Dad came outside and saw me sitting there with the knife. He looked at me as if I were foolish. I looked back at him holding the knife up while trying to be as threatening and mean looking as possible. He just cussed and turned away. This became the standard practice when she wanted to go out. Finally, Dad gave up.

By late summer, my mother had become angry all the time. When she wasn't physically abusive, she was verbally violent. She called me a mongoloid, a little bitch, and the "C" word to name a few. The list is endless, and she invented some new words too filthy to mention. She didn't have to be angry with me to whack me around, just angry at something. I was like the abused household pet. She took out her frustrations on me and, in turn, I kept working harder to prove to her how much I loved her. I just thought I was bad or no good. I kept trying harder to do better and be better for her; still not knowing what I'd done wrong.

Mom was so unpredictable and now she didn't care who saw her flip-out anymore. I didn't realize she was so drunk all the time that she didn't remember half of what she was doing. She often made a spectacle of herself and this is one of the most memorable. I was terribly embarrassed, especially because the victim didn't deserve it, but none of us ever did.

The next-door neighbor's daughter was leaving for a swim in the lake. She was walking down her driveway wearing her bikini. I'd say she was in her late teens at the time. She was a strikingly beautiful young woman with a great body. Mom really hated it when Dad watched her walk down her driveway from the window. This time, Mom started yelling out the window at the poor girl. She called her a slut, a whore… you name it. I was mortified and felt bad for her.

My brother, George, was about six years old now. I'd been taking care of him the best way I knew. Mom and Dad were rarely around and when Dad was, he was useless. Either my brother sat watching the television that had poor reception or he'd play outside. I thought it was my responsibility to take care of and protect him, especially when all hell broke loose. I had become what is called the, "Responsible Child." My mother rarely directed her anger at him, so I didn't have to worry about that, but both parents neglected us terribly; *their* needs and wants were their primary concern.

One afternoon, I was in the kitchen making lunch when I heard George cry from a distance. I didn't know exactly where he was, but I ran out of the house toward his voice. Obviously, I'd become extremely protective of him. I found him near the boat landing; he'd fallen off his bicycle and only scraped his knee, but he was shaken up. One of the boys in town pointed at him and laughed hysterically. I was furious with his insensitivity and looked at him with venom spewing from my eyes. His laughter stopped abruptly. "Don't you ever laugh at him!" I screamed at him with my finger just inches from his nose. I didn't think it was funny.

Years later, it was funny when George bragged about how fast the boy ran away from me. My little brother may have been the only reason I had left to feel worthy.

My grandmother told me how I was like a mother to him. She used to come and visit once in a while, but even she had stopped. More than 35 years later, she told me that she came over one late afternoon while I was making dinner for George. She couldn't stand to watch me play mother so much of the time to George and just stopped coming.

Now you may ask, "Why didn't she do something?" It's hard to comprehend how so many adults can become so afraid of one woman, but that's what happened. Everyone was afraid of my mother. She'd become such a terror. I know I was afraid of her and it took me nearly 50 years before I got a good handle on my deep-seeded fear. My mother was frightening, vicious, and violent. Yet, I could see she was also fragile and sick. I was convinced I had to take care of her. I had become the **enabler**.

To me it seems impossible not to become passionate with the outdoors in Grand Lake Stream. When I'm out where there is nothing except raw wilderness, I feel an overwhelming sense of comfort and peace in my soul. The flickering of the leaves on a tree, the sight of a wild animal, big or small, and the whispering, rustling sound of the wind as it moves through the trees… it all fills my senses; the beauty is unparalleled. I have found no other feeling like it. So I delved into it as if it were some kind of savior to my sanity. In the woods, I was alone and could feel safe… at least for a little while.

7 - Hooker

This was going to be a busy year for me. So much was about to influence my life in more negative ways than I could have imagined. I had just turned 11 and I was going to need a mother to help me through, but that wasn't going to happen.

Mom had now become the most irrational and unreasonable person I've ever known. She could then, and still can, justify the off the wall and cruel things she does to others. Then, she convinces herself she was right. No matter how bizarre her reasons and explanations are, she expects everyone to agree. I guess I learned to do that many years ago, but the situations were, never, so incredibly unbelievable.

It was like living under the rule of an oppressive dictator. If she didn't agree with something, it was wrong—period. She was so dictatorial that Dad started calling her "Your Highness." It only made her angrier, but he seemed to get some petty satisfaction from it and I must admit that I did too.

As far as I was concerned, my mere existence was an enormous burden to Mom. She treated me with pure hatefulness. She often ridiculed me for no reason at all. If she didn't like the way I was standing, she'd mimic me in a foolishly, exaggerated way saying, "Look at you standing there!" and make me feel like a complete idiot just for "standing there."

I wasn't her only target; she made a fool out of a lot of people—including those she called "friends"—with little to no reason. She even picked apart a person's appearance and if you were a girl, she'd rip you apart because of sheer jealousy. She always hated girls and still does. She often reminded me that she never wanted a girl in the first place. I tried to be a good boyish-girl, but that didn't work either.

When she insulted my appearance or something that I did naturally—like standing—I took her very seriously. I was just a little girl going through some major changes and I felt ugly. Ironically, I was a pretty girl. I had long, light blonde hair, blue eyes, and high cheekbones. I had great teeth and a strong jaw. I was strong and in great shape with nice legs, yet I rarely looked in the mirror because I didn't like what I saw.

Although my mother only smoked occasionally, she and many others said smoking calmed their nerves. I think it was a common way of validating the habit in the 60's. Regardless, I was desperate to find something to help me cope and calm my nerves because I was about to explode. During lunch, I walked from school to the convenience store and bought my first pack of cigarettes. Then I hid behind the store and smoked one after the other hoping I'd soon feel those calming effects. I felt a little better just because I believed the myth.

I'd been smoking for a few days and I kind of liked it, so I knew I was going to have tell Mom. I didn't want to have to do it behind her back and I knew she'd figure it out sooner or later anyway.

I figured she was going to be very angry with me so I nervously hemmed, hawed, and dodged what I really needed to say. "Mom, I started doing something. I guess it's not that bad, but I thought I'd better tell you. I don't think that it's not a sin or anything, but..."

"What is it?" She blurted out in angry anticipation. She startled me and I dropped my head and said, "I started smoking."

Mom let out a heavy sigh of relief and said, "Oh! Is that all?"

Her reaction stunned me and I didn't know what to say. As the look of bewilderment invaded my face she said, "Jesus! The way you were going on like that, I thought you were pregnant!"

WHY WOULD SHE THINK I WAS PREGNANT? SHE MUST KNOW I'M HAVING SEX WITH DAD.

I laughed nervously since I was full of guilt, but Mom was so relieved that I wasn't pregnant, she gave me permission to smoke. She did lay down some guidelines: I had to buy my own cigarettes, which were five dollars a carton then and I had to smoke outside or in the cellar. She gave me five dollars a week for allowance, so I felt like I was in good shape.

Today, I wish she'd gotten furious and slapped me silly for smoking, but it wasn't unusual for Mom to do the exact opposite of what a protective and caring parent would have done.

Adding to my little world of complications, I started my period. I'd just turned 11. Aside from all the new hormones running rampant, I was bleeding excessively with a lot of big blood clots. Mom made it seem as if it was normal and she said it was time I learned about the "birds and the bees."

I wasn't looking forward to this, but I listened to her with the focus and intensity she expected of me. I also acted as if I had no idea what she was talking about, but what I did learn was I could get pregnant now. She neglected to tell me anything about contraceptives. I just remember thinking:

NOW DAD—LESTER—CAN GET ME PREGNANT. I'VE GOT TO TELL HIM.

I'd quit begging Dad to "stop" a long time ago since it was a waste of my breath anyway. I'd become "almost" compliant. He must have known I'd started my period or maybe I was bleeding all along. I just don't remember. Regardless, I thought I was about to tell him something he didn't already know, and I figured he'd stop having sex with me.

Of course, I didn't dare bring it up since I didn't want him to think I was interested or something weird. So, the next time he wanted to have sex, I asked him, "What if I get pregnant?" He just said, "So? I'm not your father anyway." I went numb—mind and body—I was speechless and I felt sick.

I'd been calling him "Dad" since I was three years old. Partly, I was irritated because I couldn't just call him by his first name, but it was such a habit now. He didn't deserve to hear "Dad" anymore, especially when he raped me.

Meanwhile, Mom hated the attention I was getting during puberty. I hated it, too. I'd finally grown "those," but growing breasts was simply embarrassing. It happened so fast and Mom was beside herself with the bra thing.

I was going through a lot of changes, but so was Mom. She'd become very depressed. I dreaded her angry moments, but I also hated her crying marathons. I felt completely helpless as I tried to make her feel better. I don't know how many times I heard her say through the deluge of tears, "I'm such a terrible mother!" I always lied and told her she was a good mother. Then she'd go into the poor, pitiful me syndrome and cry, "Nobody loves me; not even my kids." I tried to convince her I loved her.

She bawled and said her sister and her parents disapproved of her. She cried with gut-wrenching sobs and I stayed right by her side trying to comfort her. She was acting like the victim and, as her little girl, I just wanted her to stop crying and feel better. Mom was, and still is, exceptional at convincing people she is the one who is being victimized. The truth is she victimized nearly everyone she met in one way or another.

Back then, I didn't want to or maybe I wasn't capable of accepting the fact my mother was simply a mean, manipulative drunk. So I believed her and blamed the family, which is exactly what she wanted.

I didn't realize Mom was keeping me isolated from outside influences. I was just a little girl and Mom had told me horrible lies that convinced me the rest of the family didn't like me or want me around them. She even told me my grandmother—her own mother—felt the same way. She said when I was a little girl, Gram pushed me away when I sat in her lap, but when my cousin, Donna, did the same thing, she cuddled her. Of course, I was hurt and I believed her, but aren't we supposed to be able to trust our mothers? I believed she was the only one I could depend on in the world.

I didn't know parents were supposed to take care of their children better than this. Well, my Aunt Jo had seen enough and she decided to have a talk with Mom about taking better care of us. From what my aunt told me, they were talking on the phone when she gave Mom an ultimatum. "If you don't start staying home and taking care of those kids right, I'm going to take them away from you,"

Mom didn't like to be told what to do and she certainly wasn't going to be called an incompetent mother, directly or indirectly. She hung up the phone, strapped on her holster with the .22 pistol and went to Aunt Jo's house. She didn't even knock. She barged in and said, "If you ever try to take my kids away from me, I'll blow your fucking brains out. I'll shoot the whole damn bunch of ya if you take my kids away."

Nearly 40 years later, when Aunt Jo told me this story she said, "I was scared of her." There's no doubt in my mind she was.

Of course, she told Uncle Tony who never had much use for my mother anyway. He just told her, "You stay the hell away from your sister and the whole bunch of them before you get us killed. She's as crazy as a shithouse rat and you know it!"

I became more isolated as the years passed. Very few people came into our lives; even our own family stayed as far away as possible.

Ultimately, I developed a distorted sense of what love was. I thought as long as Mom wasn't slapping me around, yelling at me, or ridiculing me, that she loved me. I also knew her love was dependent on whether or not I could keep her happy. My co-dependent behavior had reached a new level and now I was trying to control how she felt. I didn't realize how hard I tried to make her love me.

It isn't hard to imagine that my social life was terrible. I had no friends, and I felt like an outcast all the time. Then, one day, a boy on the bus said, "You're nothing but a hooker, just like your mother!" I smothered my crushed feelings and embarrassment with false arrogance and said, "Thank you. I've been wondering where I got the name." He didn't know what to say to that.

I was with Mom a lot of the time when she was out running around. She'd have sex with just about anyone, anywhere, including in front of me. She wasn't discrete so I assumed I'd earned the reputation simply because I'd been with her.

At some point, all the abuse became infectious. I started to hate myself deeply. I felt like a loathsome and worthless inconvenience to Mom. I felt like the kids at school hated me and I was beginning to understand why. I had nowhere to vent my anger—except upon myself—since I'd been convinced I was the source of Mom's frustrations.

I remember the first time I did it. I was standing in front of Mom listening to her belittle me once again. I'd heard enough of it and just wanted to die. I clenched my fists and started punching my own face. Mom reacted by telling me to stop being so damned ridiculous as she walked away. She wasn't concerned and didn't try to stop me, talk to me, or console me.

The hooker nickname at school really hurt, but I just dropped my head a little lower and tried to hide my growing shame. Conversely, my mother became well known by another nickname. They called her "The Blonde Bomber" and she loved it. She even called herself that and was proud of it.

Obviously, my mother was way out of control. She'd been drinking and partying harder over the past year. She'd been running around with countless men. Mom even started wearing her 22-caliber pistol in a holster on her hip on a regular basis. From what I've heard, she and her gun were the topic of conversation at the dinner table in several homes around town. She was irrational, unpredictable, and very scary. No one wanted to get on the bad side of her.

I can't tell you how many emotional and physical scars the family had suffered, but the fighting had gotten so frequent and violent, Dad decided to move out. He asked my aunt and uncle if he could move into one of the camps they were now renting to hunters. Contrary to what their "gut-feelings" were, they let him move in.

Years later, my aunt told me it was hard to say no to Lester since they felt sorry for him. The truth of the matter was they really didn't want him on the property because they were afraid Mom would fight with him there, too. After all, they had a business to run now and they didn't need the chaos.

Meanwhile, Mom had started dating another man and it was more serious than her usual flings. David was a big man; he stood six feet three and weighed about 225 pounds. He had brown, well-groomed hair and a boyish look that made him appear harmless. He also drank a lot, which was probably a part of the attraction. David started coming up to Grand Lake with Mom. He just brought more chaos and violence into our lives.

Even though Dad wasn't living with us, the fights never stopped. I don't know why Dad didn't just stay away. They had gotten into another nasty argument in the front yard and somehow, David got into the middle of it. As usual, it was turning violent. The only difference was David. He frightened me because of his size. Dad was six feet tall, but he was lean in comparison to the heavyweight David was. Within minutes, David and Dad started exchanging punches. I screamed at them, begging them to stop, but of course, they weren't listening. As I watched helplessly, I knew there was nothing I could do. I tried to read their faces for some idea of what to expect next. The boyish look David normally had was nowhere to be found. The dark, fierce look in his eyes scared me and the violence seemed to excite him.

David was resourceful and determined to do some physical damage to Dad. During the summer, I'd made a couple of stilts out of two six-foot trees with a couple of two-by-fours nailed to the sides. David picked up one of them and swung it with ease, as if it was a baseball bat. He hit Dad across the back so hard it sent him flying face-first onto the ground. I was terrified David was going to kill him. I screamed so loud, they turned, looked at me as if I was crazy, and stopped fighting.

The fights between the three of them continued; each one with the same or more intensity and violence. They had no regard for the disgraceful public display and embarrassment to the family. Injuries, which often included stitches and bandaging, seemed to be an expected part of the process and were given little to no concern.

Meanwhile, I was bleeding excessively because of what appeared to be irregular menstrual cycles. Mom took me to the doctor. I hated the blood clots and sometimes I couldn't keep up with the bleeding. The doctor put me in the hospital for what Mom called a "D & C." It didn't seem to help at all and I had at least one more "D & C" after that. Then the doctor prescribed what Mom called, "The Pill." She said it would help my irregular cycles.

I trusted her. I believed she was taking care of me. I didn't know how insanely abusive my life was. It was all I'd ever known and I had no one to show me otherwise. The haunting feeling in my gut told me something was wrong, but that was just a weakening instinct at this point.

I loved to walk in the woods a lot. I needed time to sort out my thoughts and try to make sense of my life. While I was alone, I could cry without punishment. I often thought I must be insane… I really didn't know.

8 - A Man with a Gun

Every once in a while, something happened that gave me a glimpse of reality, or at least a sense that maybe *I* wasn't the one who was insane for thinking that *they were*. To say the least, many things in my life were very wrong.

To give you a little background, one of our cousins, Brandon, was around my mother's age. He and his wife, Debra, were separated. Mom was hanging out with Debra and her new boyfriend, Wes. Brandon's father, Lee, blamed the break-up on Debra's boyfriend, Wes.

I called him "Uncle Lee." He, like my grandfather, was a lumberjack in the truest sense of the word. They were from the days when men cut and hauled trees from the forest to the rivers by horse and wagon. Uncle Lee was tougher than a bag of hammers.

Uncle Lee had neither visited us nor come to the house for anything until the night Debra and Wes were visiting. I was cooking some hamburgers on the stove and Mom was in the woodshed getting wood. As usual, David was standing in the kitchen having his drink and anxiously waiting to eat.

I heard a knock at the door, so I put down my spatula and went to see who it was. Uncle Lee was standing there with a .357 magnum in his hand. I glanced down at the gun and stepped back as he came into the kitchen. I tried to hide the fear that made my skin feel as if it were on pins and needles by saying hello and making silly pleasantries. I'd become a pro at pretending everything was normal when all was incredibly wrong.

"You sunuvah bitch! Yah just a home wreckah and I aughta kill ya!" It was obvious he was drunk, even through his thick Down East accent. He yelled at Wes while he waved his revolver in the air.

I simply went back to the stove and continued cooking hamburgers. Wes ran into the living room for refuge and David ran into the woodshed to get Mom. I started passing out hamburgers hoping I might diffuse the situation a little. I even offered Lee a burger. He stopped and looked at me as if I'd hit him with a pillow. His facial expression turned very serious and he looked at me with intense focus, considering how drunk he was, and said, "I feel so sorry for you. I feel s-o-o-o sorry for you." He was so passionate about it and I wondered:

HOW COULD HE POSSIBLY KNOW HOW HARD MY LIFE IS AND WHAT I GO THROUGH?

I guess I thought that my little hell was a big secret. It felt good to have someone sympathize with me, even if it was only for a moment.

My bewilderment faded quickly as Lee resumed his mission and started yelling and pointing his gun at Wes. Mom came running into the kitchen and tried to calm him down. She didn't seem to faze him and he picked up the ketchup bottle sitting on the stove and drew back to throw it at Wes. "No! Not in my house!" Mom screamed. She had his attention now, but he wanted to throw it badly and he was still poised to do just that. He looked at Mom who looked panic-stricken, and he reluctantly put the bottle down.

I tried distracting him again by offering him a burger. He looked at me, shook his head with profound meaning, and said, "I feel so sorry for you."

He scared me this time because Mom was standing there and I was afraid she'd think I'd told him something she'd done. So, I acted a little more bubbly to help cover my fear as Mom coaxed him toward the open door. She told him to go home, so he left and closed the door behind him.

A few moments passed when the door burst open. It was Lee! He yelled some more derogatory comments at Wes, and then left again, this time, slamming the door behind him. The room went silent as everyone tried to regain their composure. We waited for a few tense moments, but he was gone.

The impact of what had just happened didn't shock me the way it would most people. I was used to Mom running around with a gun on her hip, so I wasn't too overwhelmed by that. What affected me deeply was when Lee said, "I feel s-o-o-o sorry for you." That weighed heavily on my mind. Other than just my instincts, this was the first time someone gave me some indication that my life was not good, that something was indeed wrong with the way I had to live.

MAYBE I'M NOT CRAZY...

Isn't it odd that a spark of caring and understanding came from a man waving a gun and threatening the life of another? Even the good things in my life came in dysfunctional packages.

9 - A Pencil

David had come to Grand Lake Stream with Mom and they got into a bloody fight with Dad. The two men had blood streaming down their faces and Mom had been knocked around a lot. Her beautiful reddish-blonde hair was a mess of tangles and her clothes were disheveled. After a battle like this, Mom usually continued bitching, complaining, and taking her anger out on me, but this time she was eerily quiet. It was as if we'd survived something catastrophic.

Within minutes, Mom was on the phone with Aunt Jo. There was no anger or animosity on my mother's end, which was another strange phenomenon. I was standing close and could just barely hear my Aunt's voice. From what I could gather, she thought the battles were happening way too often and she was worried someone was going to get killed. That's when I heard Mom say, "Maybe it's best if I do leave." I knew she meant "move away" and I was stunned and scared.

WHAT'S SHE GOING TO DO WITH GEORGE AND ME?

Mom didn't waste any time and she started packing. My question was quickly answered; she left my brother and me with Dad. I didn't know where she went, but I assumed she moved in with David.

I literally became a housewife to Lester—Dad—and a full-time mother to George at the age of 11. For the most part, I'd been taking care of George for a long time now anyway. I just made sure he got his meals, his baths, and anything else he might need since he was only six years old.

It was more difficult for me since Dad forced me to have sex whenever he felt like it. Sometimes my brother was nearby. "No! George will hear," I'd beg him. He didn't care.

He didn't appear to give a damn about either one of us. George was often whiney and he screamed a lot for little or no reason. He probably did it for attention since he got so little from either parent. Dad called him "the screamer" and treated him as if he was always in the way.

At the time, I thought it was odd that Dad wouldn't let me take the medications the doctor had prescribed; he told me, I was taking "drugs." Mom was angry and told him, I needed to take, "three full doses a day."

Today, I think he was right. I think that Mom liked the dopey effect the medication had on me. On the other hand, he probably hated the way it made me more lethargic during sex. I tried to mentally "disappear" anyway. The medications were not stopping the spells so, as far as I was concerned, I didn't care if I took them or not.

What I did care about was not having any milk or cereal for George's breakfast; we seldom had much food in the house anymore. I quickly got tired of fighting with Dad to get some since it was getting me nowhere. I told Mom and she started bringing boxes of food and cereal.

Occasionally Mom came up to Grand Lake and we'd meet at the convenience store in the center of town so she didn't have to deal with Dad. I wondered where she was living, but I didn't ask. I just wanted to get away from Dad.

NOW THAT MOM FILED FOR DIVORCE, MAYBE I CAN TELL HER WHAT HE'S BEEN DOING TO ME WITHOUT HER GETTING MAD AT ME. I'VE GOT TO DO SOMETHING…

I was usually very focused when she spoke since I needed to hear all her instructions perfectly to minimize the chances of her slapping me around and calling me a moron for making a mistake. This time, I was preoccupied as I dug deep inside myself for the courage to tell her what Dad was doing to me. She was talking, but all I could hear was a murmur as my heart raced in anticipation of her violent reaction. "Mom... Dad's been doing things to me." I blurted it out interrupting her.

The silence fell. I waited for what seemed like a very long, tense moment. My head was still down and my shoulders were tight; I didn't dare look at her. Then, she calmly asked, "He's been molesting you?" I didn't know what "molesting," meant, but it only took me a moment to figure it out and I said, "Yeah."

I raised my head slightly and sheepishly looked over my glasses and up at her. She wasn't looking at me, but she was deep in thought. I could tell by the expression on her face, she wasn't too surprised by what I'd said and she certainly wasn't upset. I'd have to describe her reaction as excited and hopeful. It was weird, but at the time I was only relieved since I thought she was going to go ballistic and blame me. But, she had selfish, ulterior motives; once again, it was all about winning.

"Will you tell a judge that?" she asked. "Yup," I said feeling nervous and excited, as if I really had her on my side. I was so stunned by her frighteningly casual reaction; I don't remember what else she said. She was just happy to have the ammunition to use against Dad.

Then, she said goodbye, drove away, and left me standing there. I walked back home and felt numb for days trying to understand why she left me with him. Again, I questioned my sanity.

WHY DO I FEEL LIKE THIS IS ALL WRONG, BUT NOBODY ELSE— INCLUDING MOM—DOESN'T? AM I MAKING A BIG DEAL OUT OF NOTHING?

After this new wave of emotional numbness had subsided a bit, I was finally forced to assume there was something wrong with me for feeling so bad about everything.

I was just 11 years old, and it hadn't crossed my mind that Dad would eventually find out I'd told on him. I thought Mom would keep it a secret. Dad was angry with me and wanted to know why I told her. I don't remember anything after that, but the abuse got worse. He was more demanding, rougher and he often went beyond the usual sex.

This time, he was in the bathroom. He called me so I went to the door, stood outside, and asked him what he wanted. "Come in here," he barked. I opened the door and looked in. He was sitting on the toilet looking as if he were in agony. "I'm constipated." I just looked at him with sickened confusion.

SO, WHAT DO YOU WANT ME TO DO ABOUT IT?

"Go get a pencil," he said as if to answer my thoughts. I looked at him with distinct disgust and a slight touch of horror written all over my face. As I started to open my mouth to ask why, he bellowed, "Go get a pencil!" He scared me, so I left the room to get one. When I came back, he was on his knees with his bare butt staring me in the face. I felt sick.

WHAT IS HE GOING TO MAKE ME DO THIS TIME?

Again, as if to answer my thoughts he said, "Put it up my ass."

I stuttered, but nothing came out of my mouth except noise. I didn't know what to say. I knelt down behind him; I was literally shaking. I didn't want to do this.

"I'm afraid I'll hurt you," I said. His tone of voice was a little calmer as he told me it wouldn't hurt and said, "Just put it in there...it will help me."

I closed my eyes for a second hoping to erase some of the image in front of me when he snapped at me and said, "Push it in there!" I jumped and my eyes flew open. It was so disgusting. I did it, turned away, and closed my eyes, trying to pretend it really wasn't happening. I don't remember much of anything else. He'd become a very evil man, even by my distorted standards.

His perverted revenge continued through the spring. If he ever had any compassion for me at all, it was definitely gone.

10 - The Love Shack

It was June of 1974 when I found out Mom and David were living in a 10 by 18 foot shack about 15 miles away. They had no phone, no running water, not even an outhouse. They got some of their water from the nearby lake.

Inside, they had enough room for a double bed and a small table for an electric frying pan. David had installed a sink into a tiny countertop that emptied onto the ground. There was no room for a refrigerator.

After school got out for summer vacation, Mom bought a tent and pitched it on the lawn in front of the little shack. My brother and I would make it our new home.

There was some very exciting news though; Mom was having a house built. We were going to have to tough it out for a while since the groundwork had barely begun. A well had to be dug, septic tank installed, and electric had to be run. The builders would have the house finished by late spring of the following year.

At first I thought "camping out" all summer might be fun, but it wasn't long before I realized the hardships. We had to bathe in the lake down the street, which was often cold and embarrassing. The four of us were using any clean spot we could find in the woods behind the shack for a bathroom. We also threw our garbage just yards behind the shack.

There was a lot of standing water around us and the cattails and wild irises were beautiful. The downside of that were the swarms of mosquitoes and other biting insects that quickly found us. The grating, high-pitched sound of their wings whined as they swarmed our heads. What bothered me more than the biting, itching and tormenting bugs, was watching George suffer. He covered his misery with anger and he'd often yell at them. I tried not to show any discomfort since I thought it would just make the situation seem worse. We sprayed insect repellent on the screens of the tent and coated ourselves with the nasty stuff, but it didn't seem to help much. We covered our heads with our sleeping bags, but there were so many of them; some always made it under the covers with us. The incessant stinging and the shrill from the wings of the damn things were maddening.

The nights were full of sounds. Frogs, toads, owls and an occasional loon on the lake filled the night air. A different kind of wildlife was shattering those soothing sounds; it was Mom and David having sex. They were loud, almost as if they were proud to announce what they were doing. Often, we'd hear someone yell from a passing car, "Put it to her, David!" It was probably the same person all the time, but it was embarrassing and it felt like the whole world knew what was going on.

On the flip side, they were constantly drinking and fighting. Mom was always provoking David with her incessant nagging and verbal abuse, not to mention the fact she was still running around with every Tom, Dick, and Harry in town. David was very jealous and he often showed it by punching her in the face and throwing her around. The entire summer was an emotional roller-coaster ride with a bloody fistfight one day and a little peace the next. Ironically, they nicknamed their little summer home the "Love Shack."

Soon it was late August. The days were still comfortable, but it could easily drop into the mid-40's by dawn. George and I were getting very cold in our tent. I certainly didn't want to complain to Mom about it. I suggested we zip our sleeping bags together we could share body heat. Even though he was my little brother, I couldn't stop the fear that immediately invaded my entire body because I thought that my suggestion would be interpreted as having some sexual implication. Obviously, it was not—much to my relief—and George agreed. We were a lot warmer after that.

Mom and David only had a small, electric heater in the shack, so they were beginning to feel the cold, too.

Coincidentally, the two-story house next to the shack was empty. Mom rented it for the winter. We moved in just before school started.

It was an older home, but it was nice to be in a house again. My brother and I had our own bedrooms on the second floor. I think the living room was where Mom and David set up their bedroom. The dining room was filled with boxes Mom had brought in from somewhere. The only place to sit down and relax was at the kitchen table, so I gladly spent a lot of time in my room.

It wasn't long before David was taking drastic measures to keep Mom from running around on him. Beating her up wasn't working, so he padlocked her inside the house. She threw a tantrum and ended up breaking out of the house. That led to another ugly fight.

I felt like her little bodyguard. In reality, there wasn't much I could do to protect her from David. He was a big, angry man fueled by booze. He scared me, but I was getting sick of it and finally lashed out with deadly force.

I was upstairs in my room. I had music playing, but I could also hear the sound of their escalating voices downstairs. I listened intensely as I had a hundred times before. I couldn't hear the words, but I knew the tone all too well. Without another thought, I quietly crept down the stairs to evaluate the severity of the fight.

I moved cautiously through the maze of boxes stored in the dining room. I slowly walked toward the door to the kitchen where they were fighting. I couldn't see them yet, but I put both of my arms up in a defensive mode in case I had to deflect any flying objects.

As I moved closer to the doorway, I saw David standing with his back to the door with his 30-06, high-powered rifle in his hand. They were face to face and so engrossed in their fight that neither of them had noticed me standing there. I could see the look in David's eyes that usually preceded his fist to Mom's face and I felt helpless. I knew he was going to hit her.

I looked around the room and saw the 30-30 rifle leaning against the wall about eight feet away. It was nice to know it was handy.

Then, David started to turn toward the door. My heart leaped as I thought he was leaving, but instead, he raised his rifle and smashed the window in the door with the butt of it. The broken shards of glass hadn't even hit the floor when he swung around and slammed the butt of the rifle into Mom's face. With no regard to the damage he had inflicted, he opened the door and left, slamming it behind him. More glass flew from the window and Mom stood there with her hands over her face. I knew she'd be okay since she was still standing. Now all I wanted to do was kill David.

I ran to get the 30-30. I picked it up and went to the door. I quickly put the rifle through the broken window and leaned out while trying to ignore the jagged glass as it ripped through my shirt and cut into my skin. David was walking along the driveway beside Mom's car. I prepared to aim. He looked back, saw the rifle, and ran. I pulled the trigger hoping I'd get lucky and hit him. He ran out of sight. I'd missed.

Then, I realized how close the shot had come to my mother's car. I said, "Shit Mom! Did I hit your car?"

I hadn't even turned around yet and fear had already set in. I was afraid that Mom was going to be furious with me. After all, I'd tried to kill her boyfriend and I might have shot her car. I thought:

MAYBE IF I PRETEND THAT I DIDN'T REALIZE WHAT I WAS DOING... THAT'S IT! I'LL FAINT SO I DON'T HAVE TO DEAL WITH HER!

So, I pretended I was in shock and I started to lean on the wall when I heard her degrading tone of voice, "Oh stop it! You knew damn well what you were doing!" As cold as her comment was, she was right and I knew it, so I stopped being so dramatic and let my natural shock take over.

I hated David; I hated him for the rotten, verbal abuse towards her and me. He called us both whores and sluts and he said we were nothing but cunts. I'm sure he'd heard the "hooker" rumors about me and, no doubt, he put me in the same category as my mother.

Mom wasn't any better and she called me the same things. She also said I was stupid and I didn't act my age although at 12 years old I had no idea what that meant. Of course, she did need me to act older in many settings, especially since we were "sisters."

She didn't stop at that though, she even told me the pores in my skin were too big and they held a lot of dirt, my hair was stringy, and I was pathetic. I didn't know how to fix it and what's worse, I just thought I was defective and unfixable.

Mom told me I was a spoiled, selfish, and troublesome child. She told other people I was a troubled kid. She didn't just tell them either; she worked pretty hard to make people think I was a problem child to cover up what was really wrong.

There are several **roles each child plays in an alcoholic or dysfunctional family**. I played several; one was called the "Scapegoat". It wasn't that difficult since one of the symptoms is a child who 'acts out'. Adding to the mix and confirming my mother's public claims was the fact that I was on medication and, therefore, must have problems. In many ways, I was, literally, the Scapegoat, someone my mother could blame for whatever suited her fancy at the time.

There were several roles classified as typical in an alcoholic or dysfunctional family I appeared to play in this tumultuous 'game' of life. I was very angry and although I could rarely act out my anger at home, I often did at school.

I had a long fuse, but when it reached its end, I exploded. I'd get into fights, hit walls or windows or go into a verbal tantrum I often didn't remember.

Now, school was back in session and the spells were relentless. The doctors had diagnosed me with petit mal epilepsy and increased my medications, but, now, the so-called "seizures" wouldn't stop. They were happening more often, too. They were a little different because I'd actually pass out once in a while. Sometimes I could hear what was going on around me, but I couldn't move or do anything. I'd sit at my desk with my head down and then I'd feel myself urinating uncontrollably. Not only was it embarrassing, but the ridicule from the kids was unbearable. Every day someone would yell, "Did you bring your Pampers?" I wanted to die; I wished I were invisible or could go somewhere and be left alone.

Unlike me, George was more sociable and a lot more comfortable around people. He made some friends at school and sometimes they'd invite him to stay at their house overnight. That was the case this night.

David, Mom, and I were headed toward town and we stopped to drop off a few things for George at his friend's house. It was snowing and the ground was covered in about an inch of beautiful, white snow. It's a wonder I noticed how pretty it was outside over the crude arguing inside, but sometimes it was the only beauty I saw.

David stopped the car on the road in front of George's friend's house and I noticed the argument was approaching the violent level again. I was sitting in the back seat. They were verbally hacking away at each other while Mom gathered George's things and got out of the car. David was still yelling at her, so she bent over and stuck her head in the door to tell David to shut his filthy mouth, but before she could finish her sentence, he threw a thermos bottle at her. It hit her right in the face. She dropped everything and covered her face with both hands. I could tell she was hurt, so I jumped from the car to check on her.

I'd barely gotten out of the car when David spun his tires on the snow-covered road and took off.

Mom still had her hands pressed hard over her face and I was begging her to let me see her. Blood started oozing between her fingers, running down her hand, and began dripping onto the bright, white snow. I said, "Oh, God! Mom, let me see."

She slowly uncovered her face and looked at me like a little girl. She had a deep gash over her left eye. I stood there for a moment feeling helpless as I watched her bleed. I didn't know what to do. We were standing in the middle of the road, in a snowstorm, without a car. I couldn't bear to let George know what had happened because I didn't want to upset him, let alone, embarrass him in front of his friend's family.

Thankfully, a truck came along, so I waved it down. The man driving stopped and I quickly told him what happened. Mom jumped in his truck, so I had to assume she knew him. But she probably knew nearly every man in the region and, if she didn't, she'd make it a point to get to know him. They took off and left me standing in the road in a snowstorm. I was speechless. I just shook my head in amazement and started walking home. With all I had to think about, I still thought of my brother and remembered that he never did get his clothes.

The next morning, Mom had two black eyes to accent several stitches over her left eye and into her eyebrow. I couldn't look at her without feeling empathetic pain and I hoped David felt like crap for what he'd done.

When Mom got sick and tired of David's beatings, she'd throw him out of the house. Believe it or not, this was not one of those times. Nevertheless, when she did he just went next door to the love shack and then the harassment continued in one way or another. Sometimes he threatened to kill himself if she left him. Once, he broke a window to get back in the house. One way or another, he'd worm his way back into her heart and come home.

This time, they'd been fighting for quite a while and now David was slapping and pushing Mom all over the kitchen. As the fight became more violent, David started throwing things, including Mom's old, beloved, "Royal" typewriter. That really pissed her off when it hit the floor. She picked it up and saw it was badly bent. She screamed at him and told him to leave.

He left and then I sat down in the kitchen with Mom trying to make her feel better. She was pretty shook up this time and she cried hard. I begged and pleaded with her to make him stay away. She just kept saying she loved him. I felt my heart sink; I knew he'd be back again.

I knew I couldn't say or do anything to change her mind, so I sat with her in silence for a few minutes. The stillness was a relief.

I WISH IT WOULD STAY THIS QUIET. GOD, PLEASE DON'T LET HIM COME BACK...

Then, the incredibly wonderful quiet was interrupted by the piercing blast of a gun. Mom and I looked at each other in horror, knowing what the noise meant. We didn't need to speak. We knew he'd shot himself. He threatened to do it every time she kicked him out. Neither one of us knew what to do for a moment. Then she got up from the table and so did I.

I begged her, "No Mom! Please don't go over there," but she was going whether I liked it or not. I don't know what I was more afraid of, seeing David lying in a pool of blood, or having to handle my mother's predictably hysterical reaction. Regardless, I prepared myself for both.

Mom led the way as we went outside. We walked around the front of the house and toward the shack. We moved slowly as if we were at war and approaching the enemy. My heart was pounding hard in my chest as we walked toward the door. He wasn't inside. We crept around the side of the shack and toward the back. Mom stopped before looking around the backside of the building. She took a deep breath and prepared herself for the worst. We leaned around the corner and there was David with a sadistic smile on his face. She moaned a sigh of relief, reached out and hugged him as he chuckled.

He really thought he was funny. I was disgusted. Mom realized he'd duped her and quickly turned around and headed back to the house. I think she had a massive, emotional overload as she dealt with the relief of seeing him alive and the anger from the cruel mind game he'd played on her. It didn't matter though; she'd heard his bizarre cry for forgiveness and his desperate and twisted display of love loud and clear. He moved back in and, as usual, they were fairly well behaved for a few days.

That didn't last for long; it never did. The fighting between them returned to its unpredictable, but consistent level of miserable. I was tired of it and the trickle-down abuse I had to deal with. I was angry with them both.

I got a chance to vent my anger after school one afternoon. It might not seem like much, but I enjoyed every moment—well almost.

Mom and David were working the same shift at the mill, so it was quiet around the house. I decided to get something to eat. I went to the refrigerator, opened it, and all that was in there were about six bottles of booze including wine, vodka, and whiskey. The beer usually came fresh daily.

I was tired of an empty refrigerator, too. I grabbed all the bottles and stacked them like wood in my arms and then I stomped out to the dump behind the shack next door. As if I were performing a ritual, I opened each bottle, lifted it out in front of me, turned it upside down and watched the booze drain onto the ground. Then, with great satisfaction, I slammed every bottle as hard as I could into the trash heap shattering the emblem of our shameful and horrible life into tiny pieces.

When I finished my little tantrum, I realized I was in trouble. I walked back to the house and sat down at the kitchen table. I knew I'd have to explain what I'd done when they got home. So I just waited.

Finally, I heard their car pull into the driveway. As the kitchen door opened, I tried to act normal, but I was afraid. The refrigerator was right by the door. I knew that was the first place she'd go and I was sitting only 10 feet from the fridge. David was right behind her when she opened the refrigerator door. I just turned my head, closed my eyes, and waited for the pain of the first blow when I heard Mom say, "Shit! We forgot to buy liquor."

I was dumbfounded, but I was able to breathe again feeling like I had a second chance at life. Without another word, they both went back out the door to buy more booze. They never even said a word to me, as if I wasn't even there.

Although I'd just escaped a serious beating, I was scared as I now began to realize how serious their drinking problem was. What I didn't know, was it was going to get a lot worse.

11 - A New Beginning

The house Mom had built for us was probably her greatest accomplishment so far. It was a one-story house with brown siding and white trim. A big picture window overlooked the front yard. We had three bedrooms and one bathroom.

The kitchen floor had pretty linoleum with red, black, and gold colors in the design; I liked it. The wallpaper was white with tasteful arrangements of colorful fruit on it. The curtains matched the wallpaper nicely. All the appliances were the popular 1970's amber color and she'd bought a dishwasher, too.

I couldn't wait to see my room. It was last year when Mom let me pick out my own carpeting from a small swatch and I was anxious to see it on the floor. My eyes lit up as I walked through the door. My pink, variegated, shag carpet was more beautiful than I'd remembered and the walls were painted pink, too. I had sliding doors on my closet and a double bed with a pink flowered bedspread. On my headboard was my own red, white, and blue phone. I was impressed; she'd done very well.

David and Mom's room was painted white and the carpet was red. George's room was blue with blue carpet. They laid the same 1970's style, gold, shag carpet in the hall and living room.

Everything smelled so clean and new. I looked around the house and thought about all the work Mom had put into decorating the house; it was the first warm and fuzzy feeling I can remember having.

Our new home seemed to tranquilize the violence for a little while. A couple of months had passed and Mom and David hadn't had any violent fights and they appeared somewhat positive. I thought things might be taking a turn for the better, but that feeling was short lived.

"D-day" Mom called it; the final court date was approaching for the divorce and that's when the bickering and fighting started again. I guess it was only a matter of time, but David got angry when Mom got together with Dad and he also thought she spent too much time with her attorney. His hunches were right; I'd seen her flirting and drinking with her attorney right in his office. If she wasn't right under David's nose, then he assumed she was screwing someone. Sadly, that was usually true.

Dinnertime was when many of the squabbles began and this time, David had run out of words. He picked up his dinner plate and threw it. The plate full of food flew just inches from Mom's face and across the room. Crash! It slammed into the kitchen wall. Pieces of the broken plate and chicken fell to the floor while mashed potatoes and vegetables clung to the wall. Mom jumped up from her chair, screamed at him, and then reminded him of whose house he was in and she wasn't going to allow him to destroy it. "Now clean it up!," she screamed as she stormed out of the kitchen mumbling about the crap she had to take from all men in general. I was just glad he'd thrown it at the wall instead of her face, but I had a heavy feeling in my chest as I saw history repeating itself.

As D-day drew closer, Mom reiterated what I was going to tell the judge so she'd win custody. Then she said I could tell the judge which parent I wanted to live with because I was 12 years old. Obviously, I had no real choice. I was going to do whatever my mother told me to do.

It had become a nasty custody battle. At one point, Mom told me Dad suggested he take custody of just me. I was astounded— George was his only child—but he had ulterior motives and being a "Dad" was not amongst them.

On D-day, I had to tell the judge Dad had been molesting me for about seven years and raping me for more than two now. During the trial, the judge called for a recess and then asked me to go into his private chambers to talk. I was petrified. I'd never told a stranger about the abuse before, and his "private chambers" didn't even sound like a place I wanted to go.

I walked into his chambers and sat down in an oversized, leather chair. "Who do you want to live with?" he asked.

I didn't have to think; I knew what I was supposed to say. I quickly answered, "My mother."

"Why?"

I paused and stopped breathing for a moment, not knowing what to say. My mind flooded with all the things he'd done to me, and I wanted to tell him everything about Dad, but I was afraid. I sat with my head down, nervously fidgeting with my fingers. I couldn't look at him. The silence seemed like an eternity, but I finally mustered up the courage to say, "Dad touches me where he shouldn't." I was hoping he'd ask me to elaborate because I didn't have the guts to volunteer anything else.

I'VE GOT TO TELL HIM EVERYTHING… I DON'T KNOW IF I CAN. MOM WILL BE MAD IF I DON'T TELL HIM.

Then, he asked, "Where?"

Now, I was extremely uncomfortable. I was too embarrassed to point to "where" and I was a little perturbed because I thought he should have known exactly what I meant. I moved my hand and motioned toward my private parts so he'd know "where." I thought he was going to keep asking questions and I really wanted to tell him everything, but I was so scared, I couldn't even look at him.

I sat and waited for the next question, but then I realized he was through talking.

THAT'S IT? HE ISN'T GOING TO ASK ME ANYTHING ELSE? OH NO—I SHOULD HAVE SAID…

He got up from behind his highly polished, oversized, wooden desk and headed for the door. Apparently, our little "talk" was over.

In the end, my alcoholic and abusive mother won custody and my stepfather, who continued to sexually abuse me and ignore his son, got weekend visitation rights. I simply accepted the abuse as a way of life.

David and Mom celebrated with way too many drinks, but at least it was a peaceful drunkfest.

12 - The "Animals"

Mom was getting ready to go out again. I sat at my usual place at the kitchen table with my back to the wall waiting for her. She handed me a small glass with about two inches of booze in it. I hated the taste of it, so I politely said, "No thank you."

"Drink it!" She said in a deep, demanding tone as she wrinkled her brow and glared at me with her narrowing eyes. I knew better than to refuse, but I just didn't want it. I was 13.

She wanted me to get it into my system before she took me out with her. So once again, I was under the influence of pills, booze, and my mother's evil ways.

Mom had started hanging out with a lot of the guys from the local bikers' club. They had a small clubhouse nicknamed the "Animal Shack." It was only a couple of miles from our house. Mom took me there more often than I want to remember.

It was a small, two-bedroom house. From the outside, it wasn't too bad—it needed a little paint—but the inside was pretty beat-up. There was writing all over the walls, wild posters of rock stars and half-naked women were tacked up everywhere.

Broken drywall hung from various holes in the walls where a foot, fist, or body had slammed into them.

Mom usually made it obvious to everyone around, she was going to have sex with someone. She didn't care who knew or who saw her doing it either; the men loved it.

The music was blasting at an annoying level, they were popping pills, drinking and smoking marijuana. They were wild and Mom kept up with the worst of them.

The bikers also loved it when Mom left me in a room so they could do with me as they pleased. I'd just turned 13. One after another, the men raped me. The pain was horrible. All I could do was lay there, turn my head to the side, and moan in agony. Eventually, I'd shutdown and blackout.

This was how my summer vacation from school began and it wasn't going to get any better. I guess it isn't a complete surprise that Dad, my stepfather, got a job as a janitor at my school and drove a bus part-time. A lot of the maintenance at the school is done during the summer months, so I helped him clean the school floors, paint and just about anything else he needed done. Of course, that included being forced to succumb to all of his sexual demands and he had plenty of them.

It seemed as if the school itself awakened another twisted side of his sexual deviance. The school was very small—only about 400 kids from grade seven to 12—so, there was virtually no staff in the building and he could do as he pleased. I don't remember where my brother was, but his presence never stopped Dad anyway.

After the divorce, he started talking about what had gone wrong in their marriage. It seemed obvious to me, but I listened curiously to what his thoughts were.

He told me he knew Mom had screwed around on him over the years. "I wouldn't have minded her having an occasional affair, but I couldn't live with her doing it every night," he said with a hint of pain. It seemed absurd to me he'd even tolerate an occasional affair, but we know he had his reasons.

He continued venting about Mom's promiscuity. Then the conversation turned to me. It had become common knowledge my mother slept with a lot of men, and the popular assumption was that I was a compliant participant with the men who took advantage of me.

"You know… your mother is getting paid by those guys to have sex with you," he told me as if it was old news and I should have already known. I didn't know and felt as if I'd been hit with an emotional sledgehammer. For a moment, I thought he was just being mean, but he was dead serious. I knew in my gut he wasn't lying.

THAT'S WHY ALL THE KIDS CALL ME "HOOKER."

I felt sick as all the memories of the big, heavy, stinking, dirty men who smelled of cigarettes and booze resurfaced; all the pieces began to fit together.

THAT'S WHY MOM ALWAYS BROUGHT ALONG AN EXTRA GUY WHO WAS SO DEMANDING FOR SEX WHEN SHE WAS SCREWING AROUND… AND WHY SHE LEFT ME IN THE BACK ROOM OF THE BAR WITH THEM… AND THE BIKERS…

I wasn't even listening to him anymore. I realized she didn't care about me any more than Lester ever had, maybe less.

Mom often flashed around a lot of cash—it was embarrassing—I wondered why she had so much money all the time.

My emotional pain turned into anger, I wanted to scream at her, tell her she was the scum of the earth—something.

In reality, there was nothing I could do. I thought about it long and hard. I knew she'd deny it if I confronted her with it; she's a pathological liar. If I tried to talk to her about it, she'd have twisted the whole thing around so it was my fault and, in the end, I would have been the one left feeling guilty. She'd done it before. I decided I didn't want to feel that much pain, so I kept my mouth shut.

Now, every time I heard one of the kids at school yell, "Hooker!" it ripped through me leaving a deeper wound than before. My chest had a relentless, deep, heavy, achy feeling.

I tried to convince myself it was okay to say no to these men. I knew the men would get angry if I refused to give them whatever they wanted, especially if they were paying for it. Still, that wasn't as frightening as the thought of how angry Mom might become.

I felt like dying anyway so I decided I didn't care what the consequences would be. I kept telling myself, I was going to be strong and demand they listen when I said, "No."

I got my chance when Mom drove us to the landing on the other side of the lake. Unbeknownst to me—like so many times before—she had arranged to meet a couple of guys out there. When I realized what she'd set me up to do, I was angry. I was too afraid to say anything to her. So she went off with one of them and left me with the other. I knew what I was going to have to do. I had to try to overcome my fear and say, "No," firmly and with some kind of authority, but it wasn't easy since I was already afraid. First, I was going to try to avoid it altogether.

Much to my surprise, he asked me if I wanted to go for a walk. "Sure," I said as I eagerly headed into the serenity of the woods that I loved so much. It was a beautiful day.

We were about 200 yards into the woods when he grabbed me and tried to kiss me. I turned my head and pushed his hands away, "No, I don't want to," I said as I took a few steps backwards. He continued to grope at me and tried talking to me in what he thought would be flattering, "You turn me on!" But it just made me sick. I complained about the pine needles and the sharp sticks on the ground and anything else that I could think of.

I could tell he was getting irritated and it made me nervous. He scared me more when he took his shirt off in disgust and covered the ground with it. He was going to get what he wanted; or maybe it was what he'd paid for.

IT ISN'T WORKING… I CAN'T MAKE HIM STOP.

He manhandled me to the ground onto his shirt. He sat on my legs and held me down as he nearly ripped my jeans off. As usual, I just turned my head to the right and mentally disappeared for a few minutes.

When he was done, I got up feeling disgusted with myself and furious at him.

I DIDN'T WANT TO AND I SHOULDN'T HAVE HAD TO.

We walked out of the woods and I saw Mom standing by the car. She wasn't paying any attention to me as I hurried over to her. I was so angry, I forgot to feel afraid, "Mom, I told him I didn't want to, but he made me do it anyway."

Her head snapped around and she scowled at me. Her eyes seemed as if they went dark as her brow protruded familiarly over them—she looked at me as if I were nuts—now I was afraid. My anger was long-gone and I'm sure she could see the panic in my eyes.

"Oh Darlene! You know you wanted it anyway," she said in that all too familiar, belittling, and disgusted tone of voice.

I felt as if she'd kicked me in the chest; I wanted to die right there. She didn't care what they did with me. That was one of the most devastating things she'd ever said to me. I realized, then, I meant nothing to her. I didn't mean anything to anyone.

13 - My Real Father

I'd become very angry… angry with Mom, David, my stepfather, and myself. I was tired of being hurt and feeling like dying. So far, my summer vacation had been filled with Mom's "parties," then the fights at home and the dreaded visits with my stepfather.

I think I'd become a necessary evil to my mother. She really didn't want me around, but she needed me for moral and emotional support. She used me to drive her home when she was too drunk to do it herself and, now we know, she sold me for sex. In her mind, I was competition, but I was also her daughter. I'm not sure how much money I made for her or how many free drinks and favors I'd provided for her by being her prostitute, but decades later my research uncovered the fact that I did indeed serve that purpose for her. She also got some promotions at work and got herself out of trouble several times since she was often late, didn't go to work at all, or she went to work drunk. I think she converted the guilt and shame she must have felt into anger and directed it at me. She certainly wouldn't accept any responsibility—even though she was the one who put me in these situations. In her mind, I was the cause of her guilt and jealousy.

Mom didn't just lash out at me because of jealousy, hatred, or whatever else she had in her twisted mind, she'd pound on my head and face when she was fighting with David. She was afraid of David and knew he'd beat her, so she'd turn away from him and take her fury out on me.

Countless times, she grabbed my head with both hands and violently pulled me toward her face… nose to nose. Her hot, booze-saturated breath blowing on my face as she screamed at me made me stop breathing. When she finished calling me a slut, a whore and anything else she could conjure up, she'd spit in my face. Still holding my face, she glared at me—her eyes sunk deep into her head as her brow seemed to protrude and her mouth turned down with hate as if she were daring me to retaliate. I just stood there rigid. She held my head tightly between her hands while I stood there and she watched the phlegm run down my face. Then she shoved my head away as if it were something detestable. I wanted to scream at her as burning anger rose in my gut, but I just stuffed it all inside like so many other angry, sad or painful moments.

I still couldn't understand why I seemed to be the only one who felt like this was all wrong. I compared the level of inner turmoil I felt all the time to my mother's outward appearance of satisfaction. David didn't seem terribly upset with our lives either.

My brother's complacency was odd to me, too. Although, at the time, I didn't understand his role as the **Lost Child** in this dysfunctional mess. He was usually in his room with his door closed watching television. The only logical conclusion was there had to be something wrong with me, from the inside out. I was convinced my core beliefs were wrong or warped.

Then I noticed that Mom didn't treat George the way she did me. According to family, it had always been that way, but he was so much younger—a little boy—and I assumed that was the reason. Besides, Mom had convinced me I deserved the treatment she dished out and I believed her. The one thing I did know was, he was still my little brother, and it wasn't his fault. He was only nine years old. I contemplated running away, but I didn't have enough self-confidence to do it, and I quickly convinced myself I'd fail.

I WANT TO LEAVE… BUT THAT'S JUST STUPID… WHAT WOULD I DO? WHERE WOULD I GO? LIFE OUT THERE WON'T BE ANY BETTER. BESIDES, IF MOM EVER FOUND ME, SHE'D KILL ME FOR RUNNING AWAY AND MAKING HER LOOK BAD.

I started to think about my mysterious father. I wondered where he was, who he was and wished he'd miraculously come and rescue me from my miserable life.

MAYBE IF I PRAY TO THIS GOD PERSON, HE'LL SEND MY FATHER.

Religion had never been a part of our lives and I didn't know how to pray. I thought I was supposed to follow some kind of procedure that was universal for praying. I decided to try anyway. As I began to recite the Lord's Prayer from my fragmented memory, I got a strange feeling that I didn't need to recite something pre-written at all; I just had to talk to Him. That made more sense to me, so I tried it for a while.

As time passed, it seemed like my prayers were a waste of time. At this point in my life, I figured God was probably all I had to rely on. I wasn't even sure of who or what God was or if He was real. As the weeks and months passed, I needed some kind of hope, so I kept praying my real father would rescue me.

Then, one morning, the telephone rang. Mom was still in bed, so I listened from my room across the hall to see if she was able to answer it; she always answered the phone unless she instructed us to do otherwise. "Hello." I heard her say. Out of shear boredom and nosiness, I listened to see if I could figure out who it was, but she was silent for much longer than usual, which really piqued my interest. When she did speak, she sounded baffled, which was unusual since, even if she were baffled, she'd pretend she wasn't.

"Alan Waters!" She said with a lot of exclamation and a hint of question in her voice. That got my attention as I recognized the name:

THAT'S MY REAL FATHER!

I wasn't sure I believed my own ears. I ran to Mom's bedroom and waited in the doorway hoping he'd ask for me.

I stood there as they talked for what seemed like "forever,"— boredom returned—but I waited silently. Finally, he asked to speak to me. I ran to my room to use my own phone while Mom listened in on hers. I was nervous—especially with her listening—and I didn't know what to say. We talked for a couple of minutes about not much of anything. Then, he said he was going to Boston on active duty in the National Guard. He said he wanted to come to Maine when he was through so he could meet me. Of course, everything had to be confirmed through Mom, so I kept glancing at her for approval when she spoke up and said it would be fine.

I sat down on my bed to absorb it all. I thought it was strange that he'd called after I'd spent so much time in the past few months thinking about him and praying he'd come. Then, I wondered why he waited until now to find me. I decided not to try to figure out the why's of the past or present. I figured he'd tell me when we met.

Mom and Alan agreed on a date he'd arrive. I tried not to think about it, as the days seemed to drag on so slowly. Then, when the big day finally did arrive, the hours seemed like days. Mom and I just sat in the living room looking out the big front window and listening for the slightest sound of an engine coming up the quiet back road.

He finally pulled into the driveway and my heart started pounding. I was so nervous and excited at the same time. Mom and I continued sitting in the living room when the knock came at the door. Mom told me to go let him in, but I didn't want to do it alone. I asked her to come with me, but she told me to go answer the door again and glanced at me with a slight scowl that meant I was acting stupid. I went to the side door and opened it saying, "Come in," as I ran back to the living room. He came in on his own and Mom told him to come into the living room.

He walked into the room wearing a bright red suit most men would have been embarrassed to wear at their own funeral. He was tall and thin with well-groomed dark hair. I tried to see some similarity to myself, but I couldn't find any. Everyone had always told me I looked like my mother, so I didn't think too much of it.

Mom said hello and introduced me to him. He sat down and he and Mom talked for a while. He said he was living in

Wisconsin with his third wife and two children. Mom and Alan talked over drinks most of the day. Neither of them said much to me. I just sat there listening as if I was a piece of furniture. I was so bored I wanted to go to my room, but I was afraid Mom would say I was rude, so I just sat there on the couch.

Later that afternoon, Mom and Alan decided the three of us were going to take a trip to Massachusetts. I wouldn't be surprised if this had been prearranged since Mom had five days off from the mill and George was in school. Without further thought, we packed a few things and left. Alan drove his car and Mom took hers.

Mom didn't seem the least bit concerned about what David would think when he got home from work to find us gone.

We drove to Massachusetts and stayed with an old friend of Mom's in Brockton. I quickly realized Alan's drinking was as bad, or worse, than my mother's. He drank a half gallon of vodka a day and he didn't act as if he were drunk. They partied hard, went out to the bars, and stayed up late, often into the next day. I stayed at the apartment and babysat for Mom's friend's kids. I saw them briefly in between rounds of sleep and partying.

Alan seemed to be having a great time with Mom. He even talked about staying with us. I wondered if he was serious, but I didn't put much faith into anything either one of them said since they were drunk all the time. That was a good thing since I overheard them talking about going home, him to his family in Wisconsin and Mom back to Maine.

I didn't show either one of them how hurt I felt about everything. Alan had barely paid any attention to me and I felt used. I was just the babysitter. But what hurt even worse was when Alan took me aside and said, "The next time I come, it will be to see you." I stood dumbfounded and said nothing.

The rest of the trip was inconsequential. Alan went home and so did we. After David and Mom fought viscously over her trip with Alan, life seemed to continue in the same way it had before they left—one unpredictable moment after another.

I never heard from my father again… maybe it was a good thing.

14 - The Notes

Dad was still working as a janitor at my school, so I saw him every day, but we rarely said anything to each other. I just walked around with my head down and kept to myself.

One day, he asked me to have lunch with him in the boiler room at school. I was lonely and didn't have anyone to talk to, so I did. Besides, I knew he wouldn't do anything in school since the boiler room was right off the main hallway near the school entrance.

I joined him for lunch at his desk. We talked and ate our sandwiches. When we finished eating, he wanted to show me something. I got up feeling as if I'd gained a friend, but what he wanted wasn't friendship, right there behind the boilers. I was panic-stricken; afraid someone would catch us.

EVERYONE ALREADY THINKS I'M A HOOKER—I DON'T NEED THEM FINDING OUT ABOUT THIS—I CAN'T EVEN TELL ANYONE…

As I stood there begging him to leave me alone as he exposed himself to me, forced my head down and made me give him oral sex. I was still begging him to stop, but as he shoved himself inside my mouth, I started choking, so I gave up.

The following days, I decided to get out of the school as quickly as possible after the lunch bell rang. I knew if he saw me leaving, he'd try to make me stay and I didn't want the embarrassment. So I hustled out of the school through the closest door I could find when the lunch bell rang. I walked to the coffee shop at the drug store and spent my lunch hour alone. I knew he'd be angry, but I couldn't do it anymore.

Several days later at school, I went to my locker to get my books as usual. I unlocked the padlock, opened the door to find a big piece of paper taped to the top of the inside of my locker door. I looked up at it and started to read. I knew right away, from what it read, it was from Dad. I was horrified, grabbed it, and ripped it from the door as fast as I could.

As I stood there in horror, I realized, somehow, he got the combination to my lock. I was shaking as I quickly folded the note and took it to the bathroom to read the rest of what he had to say in private.

I sat on the toilet as if it were a chair and read the words of a sick, jealous, possessive, and incestuous stepfather. He had me so completely controlled. I was afraid to tell anyone about the note. I threw it away so no one would ever see it.

The next day, I found another note. The following day, he left a third. Now I was afraid to open my locker and it pissed me off. So, I took my cigarette money, went to the hardware store, and bought a new padlock.

The following day, I held my breath as I opened my locker, but there was no note. I breathed a sigh of relief, but my reprieve was short-lived. Two or three days later, I found another note. So, I went to the store and got a different kind of padlock. I just wanted him to stop.

He got the combination to that lock too. Now he was furious with me for changing the lock and he wrote in the next note, "I can get the combination to any lock you put on there."

He scared the hell out of me. He counted on me acting like the little girl he knew who wouldn't have the courage to do anything or say anything about it. What he didn't know was I was sick and tired, getting a little older, and very angry. I decided to keep a couple of the notes—for proof—and finally told Mom. She was pissed—at him—not me.

I told her I'd already changed the lock a couple of times. She said I needed to get a padlock with a key. She took me to the store and bought me one. Finally, the notes stopped.

What didn't stop was my mother using me for her own benefit. She took me to the mill when she worked nights and showed me where I could crawl under a fence to meet her after she got inside. None of her coworkers seemed to mind and the bosses didn't either. Mom could get away with a lot since she not only gave of herself; she sold her little girl, too.

She slept with most of her bosses and used it as leverage to get just about anything she wanted including promotions. She used me for the same purposes only I was a child, so what they'd done to me was potential jail time—she had them by the short hairs, literally and figuratively. I've talked with one of them—who was a few years younger than she was at the time—who told me he nearly lost his job, marriage, and reputation because of her when she didn't get what she wanted; and he wasn't the only one.

Because of Mom's overnight shifts, as well as her running around to the bars I was out late a lot. Too many mornings I couldn't get up for school because I was too exhausted. I missed a lot of school that year and she didn't care.

When I did go to school, I walked the halls often hearing someone yell, "Hooker" at me. My head was always down in a constant state of shame and humiliation. I lost count of the days that I fantasized about going to school, standing in the entryway near all the trophy cases, and blowing my brains out in front of everyone. I just wanted a little recognition; a little bit of consideration or something to make me feel like life was worth living. But it wasn't anymore. I guess shooting myself in such a dramatic way seemed to be my only form of retaliation; it was the ultimate and final "F-you all."

15 - I Couldn't Wait to Die

Now, just about every move I made and nearly every word I spoke set me up for ridicule and scorn. Mom mocked me and called me a slut for normal behaviors typical of teenage girls. I couldn't even stand with my hand on my hip; I was a little whore if I did. She made me feel dirty if I accidentally acted feminine, so I tried to act tough and mannish.

I worked hard to keep her from getting angry with me—or at anything else for that matter—because the unexpected barrage of whacks to the head and face had made me on edge all the time. I flinched every time she moved suddenly and I'm sure she noticed, but it would have been characteristic of her to have taken pride in that level of control and fear.

I pushed my anger and pain deep inside since I wasn't allowed to show any emotion. If I did, Mom made me feel worse by saying with a snarl, "Why don't you go take a set of pills; you're getting crotchety." She loved to stuff me full of those meds.

The heavy doses of barbiturates, or "pills" as Mom called them, never did control the so-called "seizures" and they certainly weren't numbing my growing emotional pain. I knew I couldn't continue feeling so dreadfully miserable all of the time. I'd gone far beyond just slipping into depression; I was on the verge of doing something drastic. I just wanted to stop feeling like blowing my brains out all the time.

I was all too familiar with my mother's emotional upheavals and the rivers of tears she cried, but this night was different. She'd been crying hard, but she was less dramatic and sadder than usual. I'd been trying to comfort her as I usually did. Then, she told me her father had molested her. She'd never mentioned it before. Then she started to talk about the men in her life and through the tears she said, "I wish I could find a man who would love me for me; not for my daughter."

It didn't matter that I'd been forced to have sex with countless men she'd set me up with, and my stepfather had been raping me for so long I'd become compliant, I was ridden with self-blame and immense guilt that still overwhelmed me. I just wanted to die as I watched her cry like a child. I stood up as a hollow pressure filled me from my chest to my stomach.

I'M A POISONOUS, CONTEMPTIBLE, WASTE WHO HURTS EVERYONE AROUND ME.

My gut tightened and my chest felt like a vacuum had sucked my soul out. I closed my eyes and felt like throwing up. I couldn't stand to look at her or listen to her anymore. I went to my room, sat on my bed and cried. As the tears streamed down my cheeks and my stomach felt like it was caving in, I tried to silence my gut-wrenching sobs. I knew my feelings of self-hatred were not going to wash away with a few tears. I felt as if my tears were a waste of time. I was 14 years old and so tired of being alive and feeling dead inside; I just didn't understand why life had to hurt so badly.

My head was spinning. I knew I had to calm down or I was going to snap completely this time. Mom had me trained well and I immediately thought a set of "pills" would help me calm down.

Feeling as if I was about to explode, I went to the kitchen to get them. I saw my prescription bottles on the dishwasher. As the water filled my glass, I thought about taking enough of them so I would never wake up again. My heavy chest suddenly felt a little lighter—I liked the idea—so I reached for the first bottle and noticed my hand trembling. I stopped and watched my hand as it trembled in front of me. Seeing myself shaking that way made me only want to die more. I picked up the bottle of Phenobarbital and filled my hand with the little white pills. David was standing on the other side of the kitchen with a glass in his hand. I glanced up at him. His face was puffy and his eyes were red from another long drunk. He watched me as I swallowed the pills. He chuckled. I looked up at him again. That familiar sinister smile was plastered across his face. His big brown, glassy eyes were looking back at me in amusement.

HE REALLY THINKS THIS IS FUNNY!

It was all I needed to push me over the edge. I couldn't wait to die as I reached for the bottle of Dilantin. I filled my hand with the capsules and swallowed them with a hard gulp. Without a word, I turned and left the kitchen.

As I walked down the hallway to my room, relief and peace immediately replaced all the feelings of anger and desperation.

NEVER AGAIN, WILL I HAVE TO FACE THE MADNESS THAT SURROUNDS ME... AND I'LL NEVER HAVE TO POISON THE WORLD WITH MY PRESENCE AGAIN.

I laid on the bed, and for once, I didn't even care if Mom and David killed each other fighting. A light smile crossed my exhausted face as I closed my eyes to go to sleep... forever.

16 - You Look Like Bob

I felt soothing warmth all over me and bright light trying to penetrate my eyelids. I laid there feeling extremely groggy just soaking in the comfort, and thought:

I MUST BE IN HEAVEN!

I was excited and opened my eyes only to realize, the warmth of the bright light was only the afternoon sun shining through my bedroom window. I was in complete disbelief. I wasn't dead! Disappointment and dread filled my soul. I felt like a complete failure.

I CAN'T EVEN KILL MYSELF RIGHT! WHY? WHY DO I HAVE TO LIVE? THERE'S JUST NO WAY OUT OF THIS MADNESS UNLESS I RUN AWAY, BUT WHERE WOULD I GO? WHAT WOULD I DO WHEN I GOT THERE? BESIDES, MOM WOULD KILL ME IF SHE EVER FOUND ME ANYWAY. (**Stockholm Syndrome**)

Ironically, I was more afraid of what was "out there" and what might happen to me when I got there, wherever it might have turned out to be. I was also very afraid of running because of her reaction to such a rejection. It would have been violent anger toward me for making her look bad since, in her mind, it would be a direct reflection on her. I guess it felt safer living in my own little hell than taking a chance on the unknowns of the real world. At least I knew what to expect—to a certain extent.

For the most part, the next year or so didn't change much. Mom never had a shortage of men willing to take advantage of me. The more she passed me around, the more she seemed to hate me, but she did like the money, which she flaunted proudly as if the bills were paper trophies. She gave me more of it too—

and she made sure it was a gross public display—as if she were hoping to be labeled as "generous" or something forgiving instead of her daughter's pimp.

I was just tired, literally and figuratively. I was 15 years old and rarely went to school anymore. There never seemed to be a shortage of life twists, turns, and surprises though. This shocker left me with more questions than answers.

It was mid-morning and Mom was in bed still groggy from another drunk. Standing in her doorway cleaning my glasses, I looked at her with the same fear I had so many times before; wondering if she was in a "safe" mood, or if I should just go away and leave her alone until she sobered up a little more. She looked at me strangely as I continued cleaning the lenses in my glasses, and she blurted out with a distinctive slur, "Jesus! You look like Bob with your glasses off!"

As my mind spun, I looked down at my glasses and stopped cleaning them. I knew what it meant, but…

I DIDN'T LOOK LIKE MY FATHER—OR WHOEVER THE HELL HE IS— SO SHE COULDN'T BE TALKING ABOUT ALAN.

I quickly asked, "Who's Bob?"

"Oh…just somebody I was dating before I married your father."

IF I LOOK LIKE THIS GUY, BOB, AND THEY "DATED"…HE'S GOT TO BE MY REAL FATHER! THIS IS NUTS!

I nearly shook with anticipation as I waited for something more, but she was done talking. I think she'd already said more than she intended to. I wanted to ask so many questions, but I held my urge to pry so I could collect my thoughts and calm down for a moment. I knew my anxiety would distort my logic, and I didn't want her to shut down and say nothing. I sensed that she didn't want to delve into this subject too far.

I collected my thoughts and quietly and calmly asked, "So how long did you guys date?"

She mumbled something I couldn't understand and then with marked irritability, she raised her voice slightly and said, "I don't wanna talk about it!"

That was my cue to leave her alone and the subject too. I knew in my gut, this Bob fellow had to be my father. I guess I still needed to hear the truth to confirm what I already believed, but I didn't know where to go for answers. I knew there were few, if any, people who knew about Bob and even less who knew he was my father. I walked away with a deeper pit in my stomach.

WHY IS IT SUCH A BIG SECRET? WHY HAS SHE LIED TO ME SO MANY TIMES ABOUT MY FATHER? WHY? WHO IS HE THAT I CAN'T KNOW HIM? I WONDER IF SHE IS EVEN MY REAL MOTHER? MAYBE SHE STOLE ME FROM SOMEONE WHEN I WAS A BABY TO USE AND ABUSE AS SHE PLEASED. I'M CERTAINLY NOT LIKE HER! OH MY GOD! WHO AM I?

Now completely lost, I felt even more alien to my own family, if they were indeed my family. Like a mere conversation piece that had been passed around to all the men who had touched my mother's life. Nothing more than something all of them could use to amuse themselves.

Once again, I began to conjure up visions of my new "knight in shining armor" that would come and rescue me. I needed something to give me a glimmer of hope—even if it was only a silly childhood dream—to help me get through the many dreaded days to come.

17 - "Paying" My Rent

Whether Mom's poor health was real or imagined, it was a fact that she was often ill, which made it hard to determine which was which. Of course, she did mistreat her body very badly with booze and pills and who knew what else, which obviously compounded her problems. Regardless, a lot of my mother's health problems were often life threatening. Her frail health was significant to me because she needed me and heavily relied on me when she was on the mend. There were many times when I thought she was going to die— maybe she just convinced me of that, or maybe she really was *that* sick, regardless it was frightening.

On top of her illnesses, she'd been in the hospital for about a dozen different surgeries over the years. One time, she needed spinal surgery. The closest hospital where they could do the operation was in Bangor, 120 miles south of us.

This was 1977 and surgeries like this weren't as scientifically advanced as they are today. The doctors said she'd have to stay in the hospital for a few days after surgery. She told me I'd be going with her. Other than taking care of my brother over the years, one of the things that gave me a sense of purpose was the brief feeling I meant something to her, and the fact that she relied heavily on me when she was sick, drunk, or emotionally incapacitated. Also, she was rarely cruel to me during these times.

We headed to Bangor and the first thing she did when we got there was find a bar to get a drink. Mom always liked the bars that were real dumps, and this time she picked a sleazy strip joint not too far from the hospital. It may have been a hot spot at one time with a name like "The Paramount", but it had definitely lost whatever charm the name seemed to indicate it might have had at one time.

Inside it was painted dark grays and blues. It had become smoke stained making it look very dingy, and it was dimly lit. The black floor had small tables and chairs staggered around a low stage. Mom sat at the bar and I sat on the stool next to her. We ordered our drinks. I'd been drinking in bars with Mom— "my sister"—for years. At 15, I easily passed for the legal drinking age of 18.

Of course, Mom started flirting with the bartender and then told him she was having back surgery. She loved to talk about her illnesses as if they were badges of honor. She told him I had come along to keep her company and to drive her home. I sat quietly as was expected of me.

Then she asked him if there was an inexpensive place nearby for me to stay. Well, it was a strip joint, so there were rooms on several floors above the bar, which were rented by the night or week and they were definitely cheap. I didn't really think she'd make me stay there. I guess I foolishly had something like the Holiday Inn in mind. When I was with Mom, I tried to prepare for anything.

We finished our drinks. Mom got up and I followed her outside to the door that led upstairs to check out the rooms. She opened the door; we both looked up at the long flight of stairs separated only by a platform between the second and third floors. The walls were scraped up, filthy and most everything in sight was in need of repair. The floor of the stairway was worn from years of use and neglect.

At the very top of the stairs was a tall man with a large build standing there looking down at us. My mother spotted him and started sprinting up the stairs like a silly schoolgirl. I followed with much less enthusiasm. After introducing herself, he said his name was Gordon. Then she asked him if there were any rooms available. "No," he said casually.

That was good news to me since I already didn't like the place. I started to turn and leave but stopped abruptly when I realized Mom wasn't finished yakking with him. She was telling him all about her surgery. Then, with a teenage style flirt, she told him that I needed a place to stay.

OH BROTHER! HOW LONG ARE WE GOING TO BE IN THIS PLACE WHILE SHE TELLS HIM ABOUT EVERY AILMENT SHE'S GOT?

At the same time, I was wondering where she was going with this when I heard her say, "Could she stay with you?"

He didn't hesitate to oblige. He was more than happy and why wouldn't he be? He'd just landed himself a pretty, tall and lean, teenage girl with long blonde hair to spend the nights with… and he had her mother's blessing!

After all the times she had given me to whichever guy would pay for me over the years, I was still stunned and actually horrified. But knowing better, I kept my mouth shut and did what she wanted.

He offered to show us his room, so we followed him down the hall to the very last one. It was small, with one window overlooking the street in front of the building. He had a double bed, dresser, television and a small table; that's about all there was room for in the tiny space. Mom looked around quickly and nodded, indicating she was satisfied. I knew it was where I'd be spending my next few nights.

I CAN'T BELIEVE THIS! SHE'S DONE IT TO ME AGAIN… I GUESS I KNOW HOW I'LL BE PAYING MY RENT!

After that was settled to my mother's satisfaction, I drove her to the hospital. We were shuffled off to her room and the nurses got her into bed. As usual, I unpacked her things, and when I had everything where she wanted and every last need fulfilled, she gave me some money to spend and sent me on my way.

I drove her car back to the Paramount. I decided to go to the bar and had a few drinks to help dull my senses before going to Gordon's room.

Gordon was in bed watching television. There really wasn't anything else to do. He was very happy to see me and probably happier than he'd been in years as I laid down next to him. I didn't even undress. He smelled terrible; he hadn't bathed in far too long, and I don't think he realized how offensive he was. He seemed as if he had a learning disability or something; his speech was labored and he wasn't very quick to answer certain questions.

We both laid there quietly for a few minutes; I certainly wasn't going to initiate anything since I didn't want any part of him anyway.

I'd learned to do whatever I had to do in situations like this, but for some reason it was harder this time. Maybe I didn't have as much booze and pills in me as Mom usually made me take. Gordon was heavy and it was hard to breath.

If there was anything good in this, at least he didn't hurt me and it was quick. I wasn't afraid of him, which was good since I was tired and needed some rest. Now that my debt was paid for the night, I was able to sleep.

The next morning, Gordon and I were going to visit Mom when we ran into his neighbor in the hallway. I sensed some tension from Gordon. He quickly overcame any apprehensions he might have had as he introduced me as his girlfriend. It was obvious the two men weren't friends, but Gordon was very polite as he introduced the man as Dick.

Dick was just under six-feet tall, had a thin build with long, brown hair. He was exceptionally flattering without saying a word. Compared to the crude men I was used to, up to and including Gordon, he was a real gem.

Dick shook my hand gently as I looked him in the eyes feeling weak-kneed. His gentleness gave me the chills. He was strangely tender and warm, and I liked it.

After the introduction, Gordon and I went to the hospital to visit Mom. We grabbed a couple of chairs, I sat down, and he sat within inches of me. He reached out, took my hand, and held it way too tightly. I didn't want to be rude and was afraid to do anything, so I let him hold it ignoring the discomfort.

After an adequate visit with Mom, Gordon and I went back to his room. I was fully dressed and laying on the bed thinking how I just couldn't bear to do it again. Gordon laid beside me in eerie silence.

I needed to get out of there and didn't know where to go. Then I thought of Dick. Without a word, I got up and left the room. I walked down the hall toward Dick's room. Fear made me hesitate for only a few seconds, and then I knocked on his door.

Dick opened the door and smiled with a touch of surprise in his eyes. I said, "Hi!" He invited me in and I explained my horrible dilemma with Gordon. He confirmed what I suspected, Gordon was mentally challenged, and although he was harmless, he wasn't capable of caring for himself very well, which was obvious.

Dick asked me if I would like to stay with him. I thanked him very much and moved my few belongings into his room. He was kind and sweet and I had no apprehensions about anything.

The next day, Dick and I went to visit Mom. I could tell she was angry with me and I didn't know why.

After the introductions and a few minutes of weak conversation, Mom asked Dick to go to the cafeteria to get something for her. Although Mom loved to have people waiting on her hand and foot, I knew it was just an excuse to get him out of the room. She started ripping him apart as soon as he was gone. She said he acted like a faggot. Her anger escalated and she said, "Jesus, you were sitting here yesterday holding Gordon's hand."

WHAT DID I DO THAT WAS SO WRONG? MAYBE SHE'S MAD BECAUSE I LIKED DICK BETTER THAN GORDON AND I FOUND HIM ON MY OWN... HE WASN'T THE ONE SHE PICKED FOR ME."

I stayed with Dick anyway and when time came to go home, I didn't want to leave. I liked Dick a lot and really wanted to stay, but that wasn't going to happen. So, we went back home without saying a word about how I felt about Dick.

I CAN HEAR HER TELLING ME HOW RIDICULOUS I AM FOR HAVING ANY FEELINGS FOR HIM, AND I KNOW SHE'LL MAKE ME FEEL STUPID AND WRONG. I HATE THAT FEELING SO I'D BETTER JUST SHUT UP ABOUT IT.

Dick and I kept in touch by mail—Snail mail, that is. Email wasn't an option in 1977—I got a letter from him almost every day, sometimes twice a day. I poured my heart out to him in those letters. It was the first time I had the courage and felt comfortable enough to talk about my life to anyone.

Mom finally let Dick come visit me. Then I started to visit Dick myself. I took a Greyhound bus from Calais to Bangor and stayed with him on weekends. I had stopped going to school and it wasn't long before my weekend visits became weeklong visits. Eventually, I was with Dick almost as much as I was staying at home.

During one of my visits with Dick, Mom had come to Bangor for a check-up on her back surgery. She never did like to do anything alone so one of her cousins came with her. Mom wanted to take Dick and me to lunch to talk. So, we went to a little Irish pub.

I had no idea what her sleeve was up, but because she had asked Dick to join us, I knew she had something specific to say. Her whole demeanor was different than I'd ever seen. She was very calm and unassuming. Usually that would have made me nervous, but I wasn't.

After we all ordered our drinks, we casually chatted for a few minutes. It became conspicuously quiet when Mom looked at me very seriously and asked, "How would you like to move in with Dick?"

My eyes flew open and sounding almost desperate, I practically cut her last word off, "Yes!"

I realized I sounded way too eager and tried to calm myself. I didn't want to sound as if I wanted to get away from her that much, but I did.

Without skipping a beat, she continued, "If that's all right with him."

I hadn't even thought about what Dick wanted. I just assumed he'd want the same thing. He did.

It was March 11, 1978. I was still only 15; Dick was 21. He had my mother figured out pretty quickly, and said he was afraid she'd throw a fit one day and report him to the police simply for spite. I blindly assured him she wouldn't and said, "She never cared before, why would she start now? Besides, she's probably glad to get rid of me."

18 - The Collar

Dick and I lived in a small room and slept in a twin bed together. The rent was only $27 a week. We had a very small closet, a dresser for our meager wardrobes and cooked on a one-burner hot plate. We didn't have a refrigerator, so we ate canned food most of the time.

We had one window, and our view was of the brick wall of the building next door with a narrow alley. We shared a bathroom with all the other tenants on the floor and the cockroaches.

I wasn't old enough to get a driver's license and, surprisingly, Dick didn't know how to drive, so he didn't have a car. Everything we needed was within walking distance.

We'd been living together for several months; I was finally happy. Dick complimented me every day, sometimes excessively. I wasn't used to that, so I sucked it right up. He told me I was a "good woman" and a "beautiful woman." He always told me he loved me and made me feel wanted and needed. He was very compassionate and caring.

Then, he began to tell me a story about a place where women submitted to their men.

SUBMITTED?

I didn't even know what it meant, but I didn't want him to think I was stupid by asking either; I usually was able to figure things out anyway.

He said the women became even more beautiful and led an even happier life than before. The men <u>loved</u>, <u>protected,</u> and <u>respected</u> their women. These people lived in a place called Gor[1] where men and women lived very happily that way.

Later, he showed me a series of books entitled, "Gor". He said they were written by a man who claimed to have been to the planet, which was much like earth only it hadn't been polluted by mankind. He described Gor as such a wonderful place, it reminded me of the wilderness back home; peaceful and beautiful.

Now, I didn't know exactly what the word, "submit," meant, but from the context in which he used it, I began to get a general idea.

In the meantime, the strip club downstairs had started hiring bands and the music was way too loud, playing into the wee hours of the morning. We started looking for another place to live to get a decent night's sleep. We found another room within walking distance for $25 a week. The room was on the second floor above a restaurant next to the Greyhound bus station.

Dick and I packed everything we owned, including a TV into two shopping carts, and started pushing them down the sidewalk.

Our new room was huge and had a double bed. We still had no refrigeration, but I had gotten used to that. We had three tall windows, two overlooking Main Street and one overlooking the bridge over the Penobscot River.

I had just turned 16 and the restaurant was hiring a waitress, so I asked Dick if I could apply for the job for some extra money. He gave me permission, so I applied and started the next day.

The restaurant was open 24 hours a day. I worked nights and into the early mornings. Several of the local **bottle clubs** closed at four a.m. and the drunks came in for breakfast. At least twice a week one of the drunken guys would start beating up his

---

1 The "Gor" Series of books by Author John Frederick Lange

girlfriend. I hated it but realized the world away from home was much the same as where I came from.

Dick continued to tell me stories about this life on the planet Gor. He made it sound so beautiful and inviting. He told me I could become even more of a woman than I already was by submitting to him and I would feel more womanly by serving my man.

To me it all sounded like a good thing because I wanted to become more of a woman. He made me feel sexy and beautiful when he spoke about his new lifestyle, and I wanted to feel more of that.

According to him, the women who lived on Gor were proud to be obedient and submissive to their masters. In return, they were given total protection and love. He continued to promise me he'd always protect and love me.

Finally, Dick suggested we at least try this way of life so I could see for myself how wonderful it would be. He never made it sound like a bad, threatening, or unpleasant thing. I wanted him to love me, so I agreed to try it for a while.

Dick and I sat down to talk about our new plan and he explained how we would begin. First, he wanted me to serve his food and beverage to him on my knees with my head bowed slightly. We were in the privacy of our home and he made it more like a game than an effort, so I played along with him.

He paced himself well. Sometimes days would pass before he'd add another facet to my new role.

A week or so later, he wanted me to walk two paces behind him when we were walking around town. He was very specific. I not only had to walk the two paces behind him, I had to be on the inside away from the street so other men wouldn't think I was for sale. I liked that part, but I felt a little silly.

Dick was incredibly shrewd and I doubt this was his first attempt at this game. He gave me ample time to adjust to each new rule, as if he were training an animal, then he'd add something else. He was slowly conditioning me.

Next, I had to kneel each time he entered the room. Compared to what I'd lived through in my life, this submitting thing was seemingly harmless. Dick made me feel good about what we were doing by showing me lots of affection and appreciation.

In time, he explained even the smallest details of the lifestyle on Gor. Some women called their men "master." "But, I prefer to hear my name roll off your tongue," he said with a flair of literary drama.

Women, or to be more accurate, the slaves on Gor wore little anklets made of tiny bells. Dick said the purpose of the bells was so "masters could hear their women as they moved about." Many masters chained their women to the floor at the foot of their beds. This was sometimes used as a form of discipline, but other times it was just where the women slept. Then he grinned and said in a lighthearted and somewhat comical way, "Maybe we'll try that."

He always reinforced each new rule with a lot of praise; like you would when training a dog, I suppose. Over time, I became relatively comfortable with it all. He didn't hurt me or yell at me; he may have been waiting for that level of ease to show. Then ever so gradually, the rules became more intense. He wouldn't allow me to eat at the table anymore. I had to eat sitting on the floor.

Sometimes he wouldn't tell me what the rules were, and he'd slap me for not following them. For instance, I wasn't allowed to take a bite off my plate until he had begun eating. Like many others, I didn't know that rule until I felt the slap. Then, he'd explain the new rule.

I can still remember the psychological shock I took when he slapped me for eating. I had always been protective of my food and often ignored my hunger as a kid, so eating was a sensitive area for me. This was a huge turning point in my emotional state and I'm sure he knew it.

It wasn't long before he wouldn't let me wear any clothes. Sometimes he'd let me wear a skirt, but never a top. He continued to praise me when I did well. Often he'd tell me I was becoming more beautiful and acting more like a woman all the time.

Then one afternoon, he came home with a small paper bag. I knelt silently like a good girl as he set the paper bag down. It sounded heavy and I heard the sound of clinking metal when it hit the table. I knew better than to speak unless I was spoken to, so I watched silently as he methodically unpacked a length of chain and set that down. Then he pulled out a huge eyebolt and placed it carefully next to the chain. Next, was a package with a padlock and keys, which was placed with care next to the eyebolt. His actions were grossly deliberate. As if the ritual was rehearsed. Finally, one more padlock was pulled out and placed next to the other.

I watched him in sheer amazement as he screwed the eyebolt into the hardwood floor at the foot of the bed. Then he padlocked the length of chain to the ring at the top of the eyebolt. When he was finished installing the hardware, he explained the purpose of it all. I was going to be padlocked to the floor by my ankle.

After laying an old, thin, throw rug on the floor, he stood back and looked at his work with great satisfaction. After making me strip, he wrapped the chain snugly around my ankle and padlocked it in place. I don't think he spoke two sentences to me that evening. I slept on the scratchy, cold throw rug that night. It was very uncomfortable and he didn't even give me a pillow.

THIS IS NOT WHAT I WAS EXPECTING; I THOUGHT IT WAS FOR SOME KIND OF SEX GAME. THIS IS HOW A DOG LIVES.

I didn't like it much, but I didn't expect it to become a constant thing either. He didn't chain me every night, but he did whenever he wanted to and when he felt I needed discipline.

I thought about my situation; comparing life with him to the life I had left back home. It was the first time I began to doubt I wanted to be there. After much thinking and comparing:

IT'S STILL A LOT BETTER HERE THAN LIVING WITH MOM. THERE ARE A LOT MORE HAPPY MOMENTS AND HE'S AFFECTIONATE. HE

MAKES ME FEEL GOOD MORE OFTEN THAN HE MAKES ME FEEL BAD. (STOCKHOLM SYNDROME)

Dick was patient. It seemed as if he knew how long to wait before implementing the new phases of this lifestyle so I'd be more receptive.

This time, he came home from work with several packages of long, leather bootlaces. He silently sat down at the table. I went from my kneeling position to a sitting position on the floor. While he methodically unwrapped the laces, he calmly but firmly said, "You are to fashion a whip out of them."

Not thinking much past the moment, I quickly thought about how I'd do it as he handed me the long strands of leather. Sitting on the floor, I made a big knot at one end and started to braid it since I figured it would make a good handle. I worked on it with diligence as he watched silently. I knew he'd be proud if I did a good job.

"It will be a correction tool," he said calmly. I barely hesitated and continued since I didn't want him to recognize my inner horror. I didn't want to believe he'd really use it to whip me.

As I worked on it quietly, I began to feel silently, but painfully numb. When I finished the handle, I carefully tied off the loose ends so they wouldn't unravel.

He took it from me and inspected it with great authority. I watched as he raised his head slightly as if to look down his nose. His downturned mouth began to scrunch up and he nodded, as his demeanor became one of obvious approval.

Then, he began to play with it by gently dragging the loose rawhide ends over my skin; it was rather erotic. He took me to bed; "love" was my reward.

A lot of this new way of life had strong sexual suggestions. I don't think he knew that I got very little physical pleasure from sex. At least he didn't force it upon me, so it felt loving.

Another day was winding down and, as usual, I was waiting in our room for Dick to come home. Hearing him come up the stairs, I got on my knees, dropped my head, and was ready for him to open the door. He came in and, within a few moments, he gave me permission to relax.

Then, I heard the crinkle of another paper bag.

He sat down at the table and I sat near him on the floor. I watched silently, wondering what was in it, fearing what he had planned for me this time. Sensing my anxiety, he waited. I sat silently; pretending it didn't bother me.

Finally, he opened the bag and pulled out a metal ring about six inches in diameter. He set that on the table. Then pulled out another padlock—a very tiny one this time—it wasn't in a package this time. He looked at it all very proudly as if it were a masterpiece he'd created. Then he picked up the ring, turned toward me as he silently demonstrated and showed me that it had a hinge, opening the circle and closing it.

"It's a collar," he said. Before another word was said, he detected my horror. He wasn't going to put up with that and his anger rose. He scowled as his posture stiffened and with little hesitation, he said, "And you will wear it." His tone and demeanor frightened me and I quickly dropped my head.

"Come here!" Although I hadn't said a word, just looking at my face told him I didn't want any part of this. I figured he was going to slap me for objecting by expression.

I was only a few feet from him, so I kept my head down and shuffled over to him on my knees. He didn't slap me, but he grabbed my chin, pulled my face up and, held it tightly while he glared at me with silent threats. He let go of my face with a sharp push. His brow narrowed and the wrinkles between his eyes were deep. I looked down quickly as his eyes seemed to darken. I'd never seen that look on his face and I read it as pure detest.

He put the metal collar around my neck. Then he told me to turn around. My straight, whispery fine blonde hair hung long to the middle of my back. Moving it to one side, he put the tiny padlock through the back of the collar. I heard the lock snap closed; humiliation and a deeper sense of fear that bordered panic set deep inside me.

"Stand up," he said firmly. I quickly got on my feet. He spun me around so I was now facing him. He examined the collar with profound dignity. He looked at it as if it were a diamond engagement ring; he was very pleased. Then he calmly said, "You are to wear it as a sign of your devotion to me."

It wasn't enough that he had me under his emotional control and knew it; he was also going to instill his authority as deep in me as he could. He randomly grabbed my collar so hard the steel dug into the back of my neck and my head jerked violently. I felt like a puppet with a mindless body following wherever he yanked. He also enjoyed giving me an occasional stinging crack with the whip when he felt like I needed more reinforcement of his control and superiority; or maybe he simply needed some entertainment.

That deep feeling of despair I'd felt for years at home was beginning to return. The collar seemed to create some kind of psychological transformation, not just in me, but also in Dick.

19 - Chained Like an Animal

I was just waking up. The dull, metallic, clunking sound as I shifted my legs and the old, thin rug scraping my bare skin reminded me of where I was—chained to the floor, again. I sat up and looked around. Dick had already gone to work.

HE MUST HAVE BEEN REALLY QUIET SINCE I WAKE UP EASILY.

I had to use the bathroom. I turned to look at the clock beside the bed. He'd taken it away...

This is where we began this book and—as you can see—how I got into this matrix of love and fear. All of it was based on insecurity and a lifetime of training through abuse and neglect with values that were extremely warped.

Because of my own psychological damage, I had little control over anything in my life. As I sat there chained to the floor, I had no control over anything except for the way I could have used that time to help control my emotions and fear.

I looked around the room trying to figure out a way to undo myself from the chain. The key to the padlock was hanging on a small nail on the wall above the old, steel radiator.

Getting up off the floor, I dragged the chain wrapped around my right ankle as far as it would go. The chain dug painfully into my anklebones. Just the tip of my finger barely touched the key. I couldn't get it off the nail. I slumped to the floor to rub my aching ankle and sulk.

My bladder was now screaming in painful desperation. I stood up again and decided to give it one more try. My heart felt as heavy as the chain on my ankle. The links in the chain scraped the old hardwood floor as I dragged it as far as I could. I knew it was going to hurt if I was going to reach the key, but my bladder was going to explode. I reached out as far as I could and leaned toward the key. The chain lifted from the floor—the eyebolt held firmly as the links dug into my ankle. I pulled as hard as I could until the muscles and joints in my leg were stretched to the extreme. I thought my ankle was going to bleed. I managed to grab the key between my first two fingers. Holding onto it with fear-driven determination, I lifted it off the nail. I didn't drop it.

Now that I had it in my hand, I began to panic. My hands were shaking as I tried putting the key in the padlock. The thought of Dick catching me was terrifying. I could only imagine what the punishment would be. Those thoughts were quickly replaced as the pain in my body reminded of how badly I had to relieve myself. I quickly grabbed a robe and ran down the hall to the bathroom. I sat on the toilet—my whole body quaking—and thought about running away.

I STILL DON'T KNOW WHAT TIME IT IS, AND IF HE COMES HOME FOR LUNCH OR WHATEVER, TO CHECK ON ME, AND CATCHES ME LEAVING, HE'LL KILL ME. I DON'T KNOW WHAT TO DO. WHERE WOULD I GO ANYWAY? I'D STILL HAVE TO TAKE THE TIME TO GET DRESSED… AND IF HE THOUGHT TO TAKE THE CLOCK…HE MAY HAVE TAKEN WHAT FEW CLOTHES I HAVE, TOO. I DON'T HAVE TIME TO WASTE AND IF HE CATCHES ME… I DON'T EVEN WANT TO THINK WHAT HE'D DO.

I ran back to the room, hung the key back on the nail exactly the way it was and then padlocked myself to the chain again. I laid back down on the floor as the feelings of extreme panic began to subside. For the moment, I realized it felt safer in my little world of isolation than taking the risk of getting caught trying to escape. This was exhausting. I rolled over on my side, curled up and fell asleep.

The sound of the old wooden door opening woke me up and horror quickly struck me since I wasn't already on my knees. I quickly sat up and kneeled for him as he expected. Then I pretended to be desperate to use the bathroom. He seemed very pleased.

Meanwhile, my job at the restaurant was wearing on me since I hated the drunks and the fights. Regardless, I remembered that I'd waited on a police officer quite frequently, so I decided to tell him about my situation in case Dick left me chained up for days.

While I was off duty and having coffee at the lunch counter, that same police officer came in. I was wearing the steel collar Dick locked around my neck. I showed him, then asked him to come and check on me upstairs if I went missing for a few days. He sat eating his lunch and appeared to be only half-listening. I felt like an idiot or some foolish child with a wild fairy tale before I even finished my story. It was the same old feeling I got when I was a kid—a younger kid—when I told Mom and the judge about the sexual abuse.

As my psychological state became more feeble, Dick became more empowered. Nothing embarrassed him either. He started wearing his sword in public more often as his feeling of superiority and control continued to grow out of control.

At home, he spent a considerable amount of time sharpening his sword. It made me nervous as I watched how he lovingly pampered the long blade with a sharpening stone. Then he'd oil the blade with a bizarre display of tenderness. Oddly, he also had a detectable hint of femininity to his movements.

One day while he was honing the blade, he called me over. I got up from my usual place on the floor and stood in front of him waiting for instructions. As usual, I was half-naked and felt extremely vulnerable. I knew he had something strange in mind by his deafening silence and his methodical movements that were always accentuated when he was about to do something "masterly."

I stood there nervously waiting for it, whatever "it" was. He made me stand in silent suspense for several long minutes as he continued to sharpen the long, curved blade. When he was satisfied I had waited long enough to have every nerve jumping in anticipation, he inspected the newly sharpened edge on his blade with blatant, eerie satisfaction. Then, he put the tip of the blade on the hollow of my throat and rested it there for a moment. I froze in fear.

He gently ran the sharp blade from my neck down my bare chest to my belly. I just stood motionless—holding my breath—waiting for the blade to sink into my skin. He put the sword down, slowly removed the thin, sheer cloth wrapped around my waist, and then took me to bed.

Up to now, Dick kept most of this bondage thing in the privacy of our room, but something changed in him. I'm not even sure when it happened, but I could see it by the expression—or rather the lack of expression—on his face. His level of arrogance was off the charts and his sense of superiority oozed from his every pore. He held his head back just a little more so he could look down his nose at me. His long thin face was usually devoid

of expression, his brown eyes intentionally cold. The only time he showed some expression was when he was angry with me; usually for something I—his slave—shouldn't have done or said. Often it was just something he perceived as disrespect or a look on my face he didn't like. There were many times when his anger and my punishments would stem from some fabricated idea of his that was intended to instill more fear and reinforce his power and control over me.

One afternoon, we went to the little convenience store on the same block. The sidewalk was bustling with people. We were about to go into the store when I said or did something that upset him. I don't remember what it was, but I do know it surprised me when he got angry. I was far too afraid to say or do anything to intentionally piss him off.

He turned and looked at me. His cold eyes quickly transformed into the familiar furious glare. I knew I was in trouble and fear overwhelmed me. I couldn't imagine what he'd do; after all, we were in public.

The deep scowl on his face made him almost unrecognizable. I stood there staring at him in fear as he pointed at me, and then down to the sidewalk in front of him. I knew what he wanted; I'd done it many times in the privacy of our room. He wanted me to kneel on the ground in front of him and beg his forgiveness right there on the sidewalk. I was horrified and I yelled, "NO!"

I quickly turned and ran down the sidewalk to the door that led up to our room. He was right behind me. My heart was pounding hard in my chest and I had a lump in my throat. I just wanted to get off the street because, no matter what he was about to do to me, I didn't want to be humiliated in public.

I yanked the heavy, wooden door open and leaped up the stairs skipping two at a time. I could run fast, after all I was only 16 and in great shape. I flung our door open, ran into the room, and leaped onto the bed. How stupid I was.

I'M TRAPPED IN HERE AND HE'S RIGHT BEHIND ME!

The heavy pounding of Dick's footsteps coming up the stairs was turning my fear into terror. I crawled to the far corner of the bed, grabbed a pillow, and hugged it tightly against my chest while pulling my knees up as if it were going to somehow save me.

Dick came into the room like a madman. He glared at me cowering on the bed, lunged to grab me, threw me to the floor, and continued to rip my shirt off. I tried to get up to defend myself, but he shoved me back to the floor and onto my knees and ordered me to stay that way. I was shaking all over waiting for whatever he was going to do to me.

Only a moment passed when he pushed my upper back so hard, I fell forward onto my hands; now I was on all fours. He'd grabbed the whip. I could tell he was more violent than I'd ever seen him before. I didn't know who he was anymore. I knew this was going to be a bad whipping, so I braced myself for the pain.

He whipped my bare back harder than he'd ever done before. It stung and I flinched each time the leather straps dug at my skin. The sound of the whip actually cracked before the sharp edges of leather hit my skin.

The stinging turned into severe pain as the leather whipped around the sides of my body and ribs and split my skin open. I couldn't just stay there and let him whip me bloody. I jumped away from him in pain, leaped back onto the bed and grabbed for the pillow again to shield my body. He jumped up and straddled me like a horse so he had a good angle on me. Then he slapped my face and head until I cried, and it took a lot for me to cry at any given time. When he felt like I had enough, he chained me to the floor.

I laid on the floor feeling helpless and stinging from the wounds on my back and sides. I knew I had to get away. I was still afraid and didn't know anyone I could turn to for help. I was so embarrassed for getting into this situation and felt like this was all my fault. After all, I had agreed to "try" this with him. Dick made sure I had no money, which made any chance of leaving more difficult. I'm sure all the things Dick did were intended to keep me hostage.

I knew nothing had changed at home and I didn't want to go back to that violence and brutality either. Dick seemed to have taken on the role of some fictional character he'd read about in those books and turned it into a reality that had become my living nightmare. The same fear of retaliation I had with my mother was exactly why I was too afraid to run now. But balance between terror and freedom was now beginning to shift. The thought of running was becoming less frightening than staying.

20 - The Better of Two Evils

Meanwhile, Mom had been calling me occasionally at work since we didn't have a phone. Like many of her calls, she was drunk and crying because she'd been fighting with David again. Apparently, the fight had gotten physical and she was begging me to come home to be with her. As I listened to her cry, my own problems faded away and the old feelings of fear for her safety took over.

I had no car and the one bus that went to Calais each day left in the late afternoon. It was already too late and I had no way to get 100 miles north. That "insignificant" detail didn't matter to her. I begged her to understand, I couldn't get a ride 100 miles north at 11 o'clock at night. She continued crying, saying I just didn't care about her, and nobody loved her—not even her kids. She made me feel so damn guilty because I couldn't help her.

I eventually calmed her down enough to be able to hang-up the phone and go back to Dick, crying.

THIS MAY BE MY WAY OUT OF THIS…IF I CAN ONLY CONVINCE DICK TO LET ME GO VISIT MOM. SHE NEEDS ME AND EXPECTS ME TO COME HOME WHEN SHE ASKS. IF HE DOESN'T LET ME GO, SHE'LL WONDER WHY. HE WOULDN'T WANT THAT.

I told him about the problems she was having at home. He really didn't care, so I planted the seed and went to bed thinking…

HE NEEDS A GOOD REASON TO LET ME OUT OF HIS GRASP. KNOWING I SHOULDN'T ARGUE WITH HIM, I WAS HOPING HE'D REALIZE A RED FLAG WOULD GO UP IF HE DIDN'T LET ME GO HOME.

The next day I told Dick that Mom really needed me because David was beating her up again. He didn't want me to go home. I sheepishly told him she would get suspicious and wonder why I wouldn't come since I was always there when she needed me.

Still, it didn't seem to be quite enough to convince him. "She might even come here if I don't go," I said. He thought about that for a minute, and then finally gave in and said okay.

I CAN'T WEAR THIS STUPID STEEL COLLAR HOME...MY MOTHER WILL FLIP-OUT... AND HOW WILL I GET THE DAMN THING OFF?

"Mom will never let me come back if I wear the steel collar home," I said with a hint of fear in my voice. He agreed with me and took it off, but he wasn't through. Why it surprised me, I still don't know; he insisted I wear a rawhide collar instead. Dick said it was to, "remind me of my place." I could only be thankful since it could easily be cut off.

I could hardly believe he was letting me go. I called Mom and told her I was on my way. As I prepared to leave, I realized how much I wasn't looking forward to what awaited me at home either. I dreaded explaining to Mom why I wanted to move back home. I really didn't know what her reaction would be, but I knew she was a pro at inflicting further humiliation even when a person was hurting. There were very few times I'd shared a painful experience when she didn't turn it into something I ended up feeling worse about or at least more ashamed of.

Still, I felt some relief as I got on the bus. I couldn't believe I'd gotten away so easily—well, in the overall perspective of things, it was easy. I felt free, but as quickly as the feelings of freedom came, they went. I wished there were some place to go where I could be happy; someplace where I didn't feel tried and tested every moment. I didn't dwell on it too long since I had to accept reality. Going home was the best choice I had at the time... I thought.

When I arrived at the bus station in Calais, Mom was already waiting. She seemed happy to see me. Getting into the passenger seat, I felt like a dam holding back more water than I was built to withstand. I wanted to blurt everything out about Dick, but I knew in my gut she wouldn't respond with the care and concern I needed right then. I was also scared because I wasn't so sure she'd want me to move back home. I also knew how well she could conjure up convincingly valid reasons for me go back to Dick no matter how insane it might sound. At the very least, I didn't think I'd truly be welcomed back home.

I sat quietly as she drove. I felt conspicuously silent with all the thoughts and emotions running wild in my mind. After I'd carefully weighed each scenario, including Mom's various potential reactions and conclusions, I decided to wait until later before delving into my problems with Dick.

When we got home, David was gone. Mom had kicked him out again during the fight the night before. He was staying at a motel until they reconciled again.

Mom decided we were going out to camp on Oxbrook Lake. That was just what I needed—I loved it out there—the one thing that was a consistently good in my life was the wilderness.

We started packing supplies for a few days and headed off to camp. When we got there, my foster cousin, Reanna, whom my Aunt Jo had fostered years ago, was there. I didn't know her that well and was really hoping for some privacy to talk to Mom.

Later that evening, we were all sitting around the knotty pine table my grandfather had built playing cards, but I had so much on my mind, I could barely focus on anything except my problems with Dick, and the frightening thought of telling Mom I needed to move back. After all, I didn't have any other options.

I sat there feeling antsy and I wasn't enjoying the card game at all. Finally, I couldn't keep my bizarre story a secret any longer. I needed my mother to know how I felt and what I wanted to do. I was afraid she'd twist the whole damn thing around and find a way to make it my fault, as she had so often done in the past. I really needed her to show me she felt something—anything—for me. My nerves had me on edge, so I hardly remember how the conversation went.

I dropped my head as I usually did before I had anything to say and explained what Dick had been doing. I waited a moment for some kind of response, but it was as if she didn't even hear me. I was baffled. At least she wasn't angry with me and didn't seem angry with Dick either. It confused me.

I evaluated her insensitivity toward me and came to the conclusion that nothing had changed since I left home the first time. She didn't care one way or the other about what I was feeling, what I'd gone through, or who'd hurt me. Why I expected something different was just part of my insanity—doing the same thing over and over and expecting different results.

I wonder if she thought I was nuts and had made up the whole story. That police officer I told may have thought the same thing. Heck, I may not have believed it myself since it was so bizarre. Today we hear stories similar to this and see them on television shows. Back then, things like child abuse were kept quiet and rarely discussed or admitted by the victims or their families.

For me, life would have to continue along its current miserable path. I was frustrated with myself for not being able to just go away and take care of myself. I was convinced I couldn't make it on my own:

I CAN BARELY HANDLE A JOB AS A WAITRESS MAKING $50 A WEEK; HOW CAN I TAKE CARE OF MYSELF? WHAT GOOD AM I TO ANYONE— EVEN MYSELF? I CAN'T MAKE IT ON MY OWN AND I DON'T KNOW IF I CAN MAKE IT HERE. WHAT AM I GOING TO DO?

A day or so later, we went home to check on the house and pick up some more supplies since we were going right back to camp. As we were packing, the phone rang. As usual, Mom answered and I could tell by the indifference in her tone and choice of words that it was Dick. This was the first time I saw even the slightest reaction from my mother. He wanted to talk to me, of course, but she wouldn't let him. She told him we were leaving for camp and he could meet us there if he wanted to see me. He had already hitchhiked 100 miles from Bangor to a restaurant just four miles away and it was raining. The camp was another 25 miles north, including eight miles of unpaved road. I felt a little bad for him, but that little twinge of sympathy lasted only for a moment, remembering why I was there.

We left for camp a couple of hours later. I know Mom purposely stalled. I suspect she wanted Dick to get as far as he could on his own before we came across him on the road. As time passed, my feelings of sympathy for him kept wandering in and out.

Once we were finally on the road, I watched for him incessantly and felt anxious as I wondered what he had in mind.

He didn't come this far for a simple chat. I'll bet he wants me back, but I can't run back to him in desperation. I do want to hear what he's got to say without giving him the impression that I miss him. I don't even know how I feel anymore. I know I'm not happy here...

We drove as far as the dirt road and still no sign of Dick. Hardly a word was spoken in the car. My little brother sat quietly in the back seat and I suspect he sensed the tension, too.

We turned down the Amazon Road; eight miles of dirt road before camp. We were about four miles from camp when I began to wonder if he'd bothered to come the distance. My heart sank as my meager self-worth reminded me that I might not be worth the trouble.

Maybe he doesn't want me back. Maybe he really doesn't love me.

As I contemplated the possibility, I watched the rain pelting the dirt road. It was raining heavy and getting muddy.

A few minutes later, my mother spotted him. I looked up. He was standing at a muddy intersection where a logging road had been cut through the woods. His long wet hair hung straighter than usual and his clothes were soaked to the skin. My heart started pounding. I was mostly afraid of my own reaction and then Mom's reaction to mine. I didn't know how she was going to handle Dick and I wasn't looking forward to the confrontation. He deserved what she might dish out.

Mom stopped the car to let him in. It was hard for me not to say something—anything—but I didn't speak. He nonchalantly said, "Hi" as he climbed into the back seat. He said he had stopped at the intersection because he couldn't remember which way to go. No one responded. The air was thick with tension, mostly my own.

For the first time in recent memory, I think he realized he was not in control and sat quietly until we got to camp. The funny thing is that I wasn't in control either. I'd have to say my mother held more of the control than anyone did at this point. Regardless, I knew I wasn't out of the woods yet; no pun intended.

Finally, we pulled into the driveway at camp. Without a word spoken, we unpacked the car. He was as eager to talk as I was to listen, but the priority was to get the supplies inside. When we finished, Dick and I went to the bedroom for some privacy, or as much privacy as one could get behind the curtain that separated the master bedroom from the rest of the cabin. I knew my brother was listening just outside the room as we talked, but I didn't mind. He was still a wide-eyed kid about 12 or 13 now.

There was a moment of stillness as we looked at one another. Tears welled up in Dick's eyes and he started crying. "You weren't coming back; were you?"

His tearful emotion gave me a little confidence, and I said, "No."

"I knew it," he said, "I took the day off because I had to talk to you."

I didn't break down and cry although I wanted to. I was fighting to hold my emotions inside; it was something I'd learned to do well over the years. I was afraid he'd think I was weak.

He was still crying as he begged me to forgive him for what he had done to me. He said he loved me and didn't want to do that to me anymore. He promised he'd never hurt me again. He kept apologizing through a sea of tears. I'd never seen him like that before.

After a while he said, "I think that this—pointing to my neck—would look much better on your finger. Would you marry me; please?"

That's when I started to cry. I couldn't hold it in any longer. I reached out and we hugged each other tightly. It felt good to have his "loving" arms around me again. I went weak as he held me. The human contact was comfort to the perpetual ache I carried inside. He felt warm and loving unlike the welcome I had gotten when I came home to Mom.

Then fear set in again and I wondered if it was just another trick. I thought quickly and decided that no one could put on an act the way he just did. The only question I had to ask myself was which was the better of two evils?

Do I want to live at home with depression that fills every waking moment? Can I stand to live with Mom, David, and their craziness... or am I willing to take the chance that Dick would keep his promise?

It didn't require a whole lot of thinking, but I was scared. I was also afraid of losing the opportunity to get the hell out of there again, so I accepted his proposal.

As I suspected, my brother overheard everything Dick and I talked about and as soon as I accepted his proposal, I heard him yell, "Darlene's getting married!"

When I heard his voice, I smiled at his innocence. My smile was quickly wiped from my face. I cringed as I heard the sour disapproval in my mother's voice, "No she isn't either!"

I was determined to get away from her and I didn't care what she thought anymore. Hardly missing a beat, I walked into the kitchen and said, "Yes, I am."

I sounded so sure of myself that I even surprised myself. The involuntary tone of defiance in my own voice frightened me a little and I waited for her to yell at me or slap me, or something. Much to my surprise, she didn't do or say anything else.

I was getting ready to go back to Bangor with Dick. I decided to ask for Mom's opinion about going back; mostly out of some deranged respect or the need to feel as if she wasn't angry with me for making a decision on my own. I was a little scared, but she simply said, "You'll probably never find another man who loves you as much as he does."

The thought of that scared me more. Now my decision was set in concrete.

Before long, everything was back to the way it was in the very beginning when I first moved in with Dick. I felt good again but was leery. I wondered how long it would last, if he'd try something else and, most of all, what I'd do if he did.

21 - Green Metal Shanty

I moved back with Dick and we decided to look for a real apartment. That may have been a sign we were feeling better about ourselves. Besides, the living conditions were rough. There were only one or two other tenants in the building and we shared one antique Victorian-style toilet. Since it was gravity fed, it flushed by pulling a chain on a tank near the ceiling. We also had to share one dark and dingy shower stall with so many cockroaches that the shower room walls appeared to move when we turned on the lights. The wiggling insects congregated in the shadows behind trash buckets and shelves in black masses two to three feet wide. Dick turned white at the sight of them, and they gave me the willies.

In winter not only the wind, but the big trucks rumbling by literally shook the old wooden windows in our room. The curtains moved as the cold outside air flowed through the loose fitting frames. Even the canned milk we used for coffee and our margarine often froze on the windowsill. We battled with the landlords for heat since they had the only control in the restaurant below. The kitchen helped keep the restaurant warm but did nothing to help us. Getting dressed in the morning was done quickly and very uncomfortably because the ambient temperature of the room was so cold that our clothes felt as if we had taken them out of a refrigerator. We decided it was time to save enough to get a decent place to live.

I took a job at the restaurant as a cook, which was great for me since I worked days and didn't have to deal with any customers, especially the drunks.

I found a nice affordable apartment just across the Penobscot River in Brewer. It was on the second floor with its own kitchen, living room, a large bedroom and, best of all, our own personal bathroom. It was a palace compared to what we'd been living in. Shockingly, Dick left the entire decision up to me. I decided to take it.

I was happier than I'd ever been. Dick was being good to me, and now we had a nice home to take care of. We lived on a very tight budget, but that wasn't a big concern.

Not long after we'd moved in, Mom stopped by on one of her trips to Bangor. As I proudly showed her around the new apartment, she started looking in closets. She was very curious to see how much storage space we had, but mostly she just wanted to snoop. While she rummaged around, tension invaded my neck and shoulders as I heard the familiar clinking sound of a chain. I stopped breathing. Mom had found the remnants of my not so distant days of bondage. I waited nervously as she picked up the chain and barked, "What the hell is this?"

I didn't know the chain, shackle, and the rest of Dick's tortuous tools were there, so I was surprised. Moreover, I was taken aback by Mom's distinctly furious reaction. She'd acted so cold and unfeeling about the whole thing when I'd told her about it at camp.

I GUESS SHE DIDN'T BELIEVE ME WHEN I TOLD HER. THAT PISSES ME OFF. WHAT KIND OF A PERSON DOES SHE THINK I AM? I WOULDN'T MAKE SOMETHING UP LIKE THAT!

Now she was furious with Dick, but her reaction had come way too late in my opinion. I felt some kind of petty, but sad, satisfaction as I watched her unravel.

She screamed, "You'd better not ever do it again or I'll kill you."

I'd never seen Dick take a step back and act so meek. I must admit I got an enormous amount of pleasure from watching such a drastic change in him.

Mom took the chain, the whip, the padlocks, and all the other paraphernalia with her. I didn't like the thought of having them around anyway. I had to wonder what Dick's intentions were by keeping them.

We were getting married and I'd spent a lot of time feeling uneasy wondering what Dick might do in lieu of the bondage he seemed so fond of. And now—after knowing he'd kept all those things—I had less trust in him. Maybe I was just desperate for some kind of normal life and thought this was my only option.

I turned 18 in late July and we got married a couple of months later on September 6. Dick considered himself an atheist, so we decided to write our own wedding vows. We simply hired a justice of the peace and got married in our apartment. My wedding band was a $10 silver band from the pawnshop.

I didn't tell my mother we'd gotten married until it was over. There was a part of me that was very hurt by her lack of caring. I guess I figured if she wouldn't love me, then I'd find someone who would. When I broke the news to her over the phone, she sounded hurt because I hadn't invited her. That wasn't the response I was expecting. I thought she'd be upset about me marrying him at all.

Once again, it appeared my life had taken a turn for the better. We were able to pay the bills and could afford to go out once a month. Our monthly entertainment was taking a cab to a local club, listening to live music, and having two or three drinks.

I was living a pleasantly quiet life and Dick was treating me better than he ever had. Although I didn't know what it was like to be treated properly, this was a lot better than anything I'd experienced before and I was happy.

About four months after we were married, the bookbinding company Dick was working for went out of business. He started collecting unemployment while he looked for work. He scoured the want ads and went on interviews but couldn't get a job. His unemployment would run out soon, and we needed to do something.

Finally, he decided to cut his long hair hoping it would improve his appearance and help land a job. He continued looking, but still couldn't find work. Of course, he didn't have a driver's license, but I didn't think of that at the time.

All I knew was that we had to try something else. I suggested we move up north and apply at the paper mill where my mother and most of my family worked. I also knew Mom had made some "connections" with the decision makers over the years. I figured she could help him get in the door.

Dick reluctantly agreed to talk to Mom. We packed a few things and made the trip up to my mother's house in Princeton. She agreed to talk to one of the bigwigs at the mill and was able to get Dick a low-level job.

Dick and I lived with Mom and David until we could get a place of our own. It wasn't easy. Mom made life unpleasant with daily snide and degrading remarks about Dick or me depending upon her mood.

We'd spent a very chilly winter since Mom kept the house abnormally cold often turning the heat off at night with only the wood stove in the cellar to keep us warm. Now, it was spring and most of the snow had melted and was gradually replaced with the usual thick layer of earthy mud.

There was an old camper-trailer up the road with a for sale sign on it. It wasn't much, it was extremely old and rundown. Mom bought it for us for a few hundred bucks. Dick was making good money and I had no idea what he did with it. I guess I didn't think it was my place to ask, but it seemed like he should have been able to buy the trailer himself. It's possible that Mom just wanted us out of the house badly enough to spend the money.

Some years earlier, Mom bought several acres of land surrounding the house. Just down the hill from her house was where we planned to put the trailer.

That old trailer had been sitting in the same spot for many years and the wheels had embedded themselves up to the axles in the soft, muddy soil. We hooked up the pickup truck to the old relic and prepared to pull it away. Mom slowly accelerated and the trailer let out a hair-raising, metallic groan as the aging metal camper-trailer began to move. I was expecting it to fall apart as it was pulled from the muck it had become glued into. I was surprised to see it clumsily wobble out of its mire and onto the road.

We still had to haul it about a mile or so down the road to the lot in one piece. We followed in Mom's car watching the trailer literally shimmy down the road. It began to wiggle and wobble as if it were held together with staples. I expected it to collapse into a pile of scrap metal all over the road in front of us. Miraculously, the green metal shanty we were now going to call home had survived the torture of the trip. We parked it on its new lot in one piece and began to move our things in immediately.

The living conditions were a little rough, but our mental well-being was improving by the minute as we settled into our own environment. With no running water and no toilet, we bought a portable, chemical toilet to use. We got water from the outside faucet at my mother's house by the five-gallon bucket.

Living in the middle of the wilderness made it almost impossible to survive without a car, especially with Dick working four miles away. Mom was buying a new car, so she sold us her old one for $500. We paid her over a period of several months. The car was in good shape and it ran well. Best of all, Dick didn't have to hitch a ride to work every day.

This is when Dick told me his father once offered to teach him how to drive, but he never wanted to learn. I couldn't imagine it. I was quickly learning that Dick had very few skills. I was going to have to either teach him or do a lot of things or do it all myself. Little did I know just how much work it was going to be.

22 - Just Plain Lazy

I grew up learning fast by doing a multitude of things like cutting and splitting wood, fixing cars, and building things. When I realized that Dick didn't know how to do much and rarely had the capacity to figure things out when confronted with a situation, I was surprised. The day we needed to fill the car with gas was when I realized that I was going to have to be the muscles and the brains when it came to fixing and repairing anything.

I parked the car next to the pump at the gas station. I'd barely gotten the car in park when Dick surprised me by getting out to pump the gas. That kind of initiative from him was unusual.

Anyway, I waited in the driver's seat. I could hear the nozzle clanking around in the rear. I assumed he was having a little trouble since it was a new car to us. The metal-to-metal clinking sounds continued for at least a minute.

WHAT IS HE DOING BACK THERE?

I decided to get out to see what the problem was, but as I was about to open the door, he came to my window and asked if I'd show him how to use the pump. I got out without saying a word. I was embarrassed in front of all the mechanics I'd grown up around and I assumed he probably felt foolish too, so I didn't make any comments.

Our new home had its inconveniences, but the peace and quiet was a comforting change. We couldn't escape completely though. Occasionally our serenity was still shattered by our unpredictably hostile neighbors.

It was a lovely spring afternoon. The birds were singing and the breeze sent a soft whisper through the tops of the trees as the leaves rustled lightly. Suddenly the relaxing sounds were broken by gunfire coming from Mom's house. I looked at Dick wide-eyed wondering if they were having a fight or had just decided to target practice in the back yard. We sat in silence and listened, then we heard what sounded like a moose running through the woods toward our trailer.

We both had a puzzled look on our faces that was quickly wiped away by the sound of another gunshot. I jumped up and ran outside and Dick followed. That's when David came plowing through the trees yelling, "She's shooting at me."

Without hesitation Dick said, "Well then, get the hell out of here; I don't want her coming down here shooting a rifle like a wild woman."

David was drunk and when he saw the look of fear on Dick's face he laughed with the deep, airy chuckle I'd always found amusing.

I felt bad for David as he headed toward the road and back up the hill toward home, but I didn't want to get involved either. We tried to stay out of their troublesome lives as much as possible since it was always a lose-lose situation.

Meanwhile, Dick was still working on a three-month probation period. This meant management would have to evaluate his work before making a final decision on his permanent employment. He was making decent money and we started to save for a new place to live. A house would have been great, but we would have been happy just to get into an apartment or something.

Apparently, Dick was having a little trouble on the job. As I mentioned before, he was an atheist and one of his foremen at the mill was a member of the Jehovah's Witness faith. According to Dick they'd discussed religion and, of course, they didn't agree. Dick didn't always come across as the most likable guy and, much to my dismay, he often said he liked it that way. When I commented on how unfriendly he seemed, he acted amused, almost proud. His way of expressing his opinion was often offensive, but he didn't care. I'm sure he'd offended his foreman during the religious discussion and that came with consequences.

When Dick's boss filed his 90 day evaluation, the mill terminated him. Dick decided to go to his union delegate and fight the decision. As the union investigated the case, they found that someone had altered the reports of Dick's job performance to support the decision to terminate him.

The union decided to take the case to arbitration. In the meantime, Dick would have to draw unemployment again. As long as we could pay the bills, I wasn't too worried. The union was fighting for his job and we hoped he'd have it back soon.

These cases can take a while and Maine's short summer had come and gone. The last of the brilliantly colored leaves had fallen, and winter was approaching fast. We had a little gas heater in the front of the trailer, which kept the top half very warm. As temperatures dipped into the single digits we could hardly keep our feet on the floor because it felt like ice.

In the back of the trailer, ice crystals coated the walls from the floor and up two to three feet. Our bunkbed was so cold; our blankets froze to the wall. We couldn't pull them off without ripping them, so they stayed stuck there all winter. In the spring, I found a hole in the bottom of the trailer directly under the bed.

We had a lot of snow that year. One snowstorm dumped a hefty five feet on us. I didn't mind shoveling, but quickly learned that Dick was just plain lazy. I was just discovering some things about my husband I didn't care for. He tried it, but I ended up doing all the shoveling that winter.

Nearly a year later, the union won the wrongful termination case and Dick got his job back. It was 1982. He got all the back pay, too. Now, we had enough money to buy a newer car and put a down-payment on our own home.

We found a little two-story, two-bedroom house in Woodland near the mill. It had no basement, but the price was right. The house had been empty for a while and had signs of neglect, so it needed some work.

There was a severe leak in the roof and it had bowed the living room paneling along the stairway. We bought roofing materials and I began to remove the old roof. I spent every day on the roof until it was done. Dick occasionally brought some of the materials from the ground up the ladder when he was feeling ambitious.

The next project was to get firewood prepared for winter. I suggested we buy tree-length logs to cut up ourselves. We bought a chainsaw and I showed Dick how to use it so he could help. When the wood was delivered, he made a few cuts, then stopped saying he was allergic to sawdust. The only thing he was allergic to was work.

The following summer, I started to paint the outside of the house. I kept working by myself, but I was beginning to feel some serious resentment toward Dick because he wouldn't do anything. He came home from work, had a beer or two and as far as he was concerned, that was the end of his day. After a few days of painting, I asked if he'd help me. He said, "Oh, but you're doing such a good job on your own." I just gave up on him.

When the summer chores were done, I went back to cleaning and being a typical housewife. I always kept on top of the housework, so there wasn't really a lot to do. I was bored.

Fortunately, I became friends with one of our neighbors, Jackie. She was about 15 years older than I was, so I often looked to her for advice and guidance.

Dick needed to keep tabs on me at all times. When I was visiting with Jackie, he'd call to check on me within a half-hour or so. The farthest I strayed from home was to play bingo with Jackie, but he usually came along.

We'd been living in our new home for about two years and already I felt like a middle-aged woman. I was only 21. Depression was setting in and I had to do something. I told Dick about my increasing boredom hoping to stir him up enough to take me out to dinner… or something.

Then I thought that it would be great if I got a job, but Dick  wasn't very enthusiastic about my idea. He didn't want me to have any independence. He did agree the extra money would be good along with giving me something to do in the winters when it was too cold to do outside work. After some fancy pleading, he agreed to let me look for a job as long as working didn't interfere with my "household duties."

I decided to apply at a department store in Calais about 10 miles away. I got hired as a cashier and worked nights until about 10 o'clock. The job was rewarding and I made some new friends, too.

After about six months, a job opened up for a floor manager in the Men's, Boy's, and Jr. Boy's departments. I wanted the job, so I applied and got the position.

I'd been pretending for some time that I felt good about myself, but it was purely a façade of self-confidence. Now it was becoming more natural and real. I began to learn that I really was a good person who was worthy of appreciation. I made friends with my co-workers and, unlike at home, I felt appreciated for my efforts. I really liked my job, my co-workers and, most of all; I was beginning to like myself.

The only bad side effect to this positive change came when I began to realize more and more how unfulfilling my marriage was. I was very unhappy at home. We did absolutely nothing except exist day in and day out. We hardly even talked anymore. We hadn't made friends as a couple and didn't socialize together.

There were other little things that alone seemed trivial, but when I added it all up, I realized Dick was as lackadaisical in the marriage as he was in his efforts to do anything to help around the house and yard. For instance, I remember asking him for a simple little stuffed animal for my birthday. It wasn't much, but

I really liked the darned thing. Well, my birthday came and went, and I ended up buying it for myself. I wasn't a demanding wife by any means. I rarely asked for anything, so I was hurt because he didn't try just a little once in a while.

Over the next year or so, Jackie knew I was growing increasingly unhappy in my life with Dick. "You can do a lot better than that," she said. "Don't you think?"

The truth was I never thought I could do any better, but now I was beginning to wonder.

23 - Who is my Real Father?

Once again, the sadness in my life made me think about the mysterious man named Bob—the man I looked like—the man I knew was my father. I purposely waited seven years—until I was 21 one years old—to ask Mom about him. For some reason, age was always a big thing with my mother, and I figured she'd tell me the truth if I asked now.

Mom was visiting one afternoon. I decided it was as good a time as any. It was one of the tensest moments I'd experienced in a long time. The tone of my voice was extremely serious when I asked, "Mom, who's my real father?"

Too afraid to look at her, I held my breath waiting for her response. Then, she let out a heavy sigh. It seemed to fill the room with tension and relief at the same time. With a bit of hesitation, she began to talk. It was as if she wanted to get rid of the burden and the secret she'd carried for more than 20 years.

"I'll tell you, but you have to promise that you'll never look for him. You'll just ruin his life because he doesn't even know you exist," she said with a hint of desperation.

Instantly, I felt pain and guilt thinking I'd already ruined her life just by being born.

I lied, promising her I wouldn't look for him. Then, she started to tell me the story:

"His name is Bob Deacon. He was only 16 years old when we met. I was living in Waltham, Massachusetts, with your Aunt Anna then. He lied to me and said he was 18; I was only 18. He was tall, handsome and he looked 18, so I had no reason to doubt him. We only dated for about six weeks, but I fell in love with him and I've never forgotten him. As a matter of fact, your Auntie Flo (she grew up with Mom and now lives in another state) and I still talk about him every summer when she comes up here. Anyway, his mother found out about my age—not that I tried to hide it—and she sent the police to my apartment one night. They were looking for Bob. He wasn't there, but they had a message for me. They told me if I continued to see him, Bob's mother would press charges for statutory rape because he was only 16 years old. I was shocked. That was the first time I heard his true age and I told the police that. Anyway, I was pregnant with you and decided it was best he never knew. I figured, what could he do at the age of 16 and still in school? So, I married my ex-boyfriend, Alan, and he claimed you as his own."

I was speechless. That was one hell of a story and I needed time to absorb it all. I had to remember detail if I was going to find him.

My mother's story left me full of questions. I didn't dare ask her anything else since she made me promise not to look for him. I think deep-down she knew I would, but I couldn't let her know it. I didn't know who I could ask about my real father. I figured—at least for now—I'd have to find the answers on my own.

I decided to find my real father as soon as possible. I needed to know who he was and I felt it was his right to know me, too. Now I had to tell Dick my intentions. I didn't expect to have to ask for permission to find my own father and, for once, I wasn't asking.

As I suspected, Dick didn't want me to find him. Regardless, this was important to me and, for once, I didn't care what Dick didn't want me to do.

I began my search the only way I knew how, by making phone calls. First, I got the numbers for all the Deacon families in the Waltham, Massachusetts, area. There were about five on my list. I was excited and nervous. Picking up the phone, I thought about what to say. Then, I hung up. I really had no idea how to approach this—delicately, if it were possible. After much thought, I decided the first thing I had to do was find out if a Bob

Deacon even lived there. If not, I would simply ask if they knew Bob Deacon.

I picked the phone up again and dialed the first number on the list. I didn't have to explain why I was looking for him as I went through the first four numbers with no success. Each person I spoke with was pleasant and tried to be helpful.

I was a little disheartened as I looked at the last number on my list. I picked up the phone and dialed as if it were my last thread of hope. A woman answered and I casually asked for Bob Deacon. "He isn't here right now. What's this all about?" she said.

My heart nearly stopped. I was stunned and didn't have time to think, so I said, "I have reason to believe he's my father."

Without hesitation, she sharply said, "Your mother was nothing but a slut and a whore and you could be anybody's kid."

She hung up and I sat in my chair with the phone still up to my ear listening to a dial tone with my jaw hanging. I slowly hung up.

I DIDN'T EVEN TELL HER WHO MY MOTHER WAS, SO SHE COULDN'T HAVE MADE AN INFORMED JUDGMENT LIKE THAT— ALTHOUGH IT WAS TRUE. I DON'T KNOW WHO THIS WOMAN IS OR IF SHE'S EVEN RELATED TO MY FATHER. SHE MIGHT BE HIS WIFE; I CAN'T EVEN GUESS HOW OLD SHE IS. SHE COULD BE AN OVERPROTECTIVE MOTHER FOR ALL I KNOW; SHE COULD HAVE BEEN ANYONE.

I decided to call again, but this time I'd do it in the early morning hours instead of mid-day since the phone rang nearly 10 times before she picked up. I figured around 6:30 in the morning could possibly be the time before he went to work and I might get lucky enough to get him to answer.

After Dick went to work the next morning, I made the call. I let it ring about five times and hung up

NOW WHAT DO I DO? I DON'T KNOW WHAT I CAN DO. I WANT TO CALL THAT WOMAN AGAIN—WHOEVER SHE IS—AND TRY TO EXPLAIN, BUT IT WON'T DO ANY GOOD. IF I REALLY WANT TO FIND HIM, I'LL HAVE TO GO TO WALTHAM TO LOOK FOR HIM. IF I COULD ONLY SEE

HIM IN PERSON, HE MIGHT TALK TO ME. THIS PHONE-TAG THING ISN'T WORKING. THERE'S NO WAY IN HELL DICK WOULD LET ME DO THAT AND MOM... WELL THAT'S JUST ANOTHER PROBLEM.

I knew there was nothing I could do right then without causing trouble in my own home and I certainly didn't want Mom to find out I was looking for my father. I had no support from anyone and I couldn't tell anyone what my intentions were. I wasn't sure how I was going to do it, but I knew I would look for him again one day. For now, I'd wait for the opportunity and remain a good little wife and daughter.

24 - The Damn Flowers

For years, I had extremely painful menstrual cycles, but now it was becoming unbearable. I had seen several doctors and they prescribed pain pills—which were not helping much—and told me, "It's all in your head."

One night Dick woke me up because I was crying in my sleep. I was in excruciating pain. I got up but couldn't stand, so I crawled to the bathroom.

The pain had even become a problem at work. I could hardly stand up when the pain hit. Several times, I had to ask my boss if I could lie down in the employee lounge. Work wasn't going to be a problem much longer anyway, since the store had filed bankruptcy and was going to close.

In the meantime, I had gone to the hospital several times when the pain got really bad. I always got the same run-around, "It's all in your head. These pain pills will do it." Or, "It can't be that bad."

Well, the painkillers were useless, and it was "that bad."

Part of my dissatisfaction with Dick was probably because of the pain during sex; sometimes I'd even cry. Why that wouldn't stop him, I don't know. Why I kept doing it is an even a bigger concern. I felt like I had to—it was my obligation—and if I didn't, I felt guilty.

I was out of work now and had plenty of time on my hands. Tired of the pain, I made an appointment with a gynecologist in Bangor. I didn't care that it was 100 miles away. The doctors I'd been seeing proved worthless.

The doctor performed exploratory surgery to confirm his suspicion of **Endometriosis**. I assumed it had been caused by Lester and my mother's paying customers raping me from the age of 10.

The choices for curing endometriosis at the time were either a hysterectomy or taking birth control pills until menopause. I already had my tubes tied to prevent a pregnancy because Dick hated kids. The pill wasn't good for me, especially since I smoked three packs of cigarettes a day and had no intentions of quitting, so I decided to have the hysterectomy.

In the early 1980's, this was a major surgery and I had to be at the hospital a day before the procedure. Mom drove and Dick came with us since I was going to be admitted for about five days. They spent the day with me and then went back home.

The day after surgery, Mom called my room. I remember speaking to her briefly, but I was still very groggy. When I finally woke, I saw flowers and a stuffed mother bunny holding a baby bunny on the nightstand. There were also several cards, which I anxiously opened.

One of the cards, the flowers, and the bunnies were from Mom. There were cards from my Aunt and Uncle, my grandparents—the whole family. After reading them, I looked around for the one from Dick—there wasn't one. I kept looking, thinking I missed one, or a note, or maybe it had fallen on the floor or something. There was nothing. It really hurt me. We'd been together for nine years now—married for six of them. He usually forgot birthdays, anniversaries, and things like that, but how could he forget—no—how could he ignore this?

I didn't even mention it to him. I was convinced he just didn't give a damn anymore, or worse, maybe he never did.

It was time to go home; I didn't want to. Regardless, the doctor said I couldn't have intercourse for the next six weeks until he re-examined me again.

Dick set up an old army cot we had in the living room for me to sleep on. I thought it would be best to sleep in separate beds until I healed more. Besides, not only did I not want to have sex with him anymore, I didn't even want to sleep with him.

Even though I knew it was too late to do anything to save this desolate marriage, I couldn't accept it without trying to do something. I decided to talk to Dick about how I was feeling to see if he was willing to put some effort into our relationship.

I told him how hurt I was when he didn't send me just a simple card while I was in the hospital. I told him about how I felt when we had sex and how I cringed every time he touched me. I knew it was going to hurt him, but I was hurting, too. I couldn't take any more.

He promised to try to make it work. Dick even attempted to learn how to dance so we could go out once in a while. We never did, but it was the intended idea.

Not much changed in our relationship over the next six weeks. Now I knew there was nothing either one of us could do to heal the damage.

I slept on the cot for the entire six weeks. Then, I went to Bangor for my check-up by myself. The doctor okayed me to have intercourse and said everything had healed well.

As I headed for home, my heart sank. I felt terrible about going back to him:

I'M GOING TO HAVE TO TELL HIM WE CAN HAVE SEX, BUT I CAN'T DO IT. HOW THE HELL AM I GOING TO HANDLE THIS?

The two-hour drive gave me a lot of time to think. I drove slower than usual.

WHY—IF YOU'RE SO DAMNED UNHAPPY—DON'T YOU JUST LEAVE?

That's when I realized, I was afraid.

WHAT ARE YOU AFRAID OF?

The discussion with myself continued...

YOU'LL BE ALL ALONE.

SO WHAT! YOU'RE ALL ALONE NOW. YOU JUST LIVE—NO, YOU DON'T EVEN LIVE—YOU RESIDE IN THE SAME HOUSE WITH HIM LIKE ROOMMATES.

BUT WHAT IF YOU NEVER FIND SOMEONE TO LOVE YOU AGAIN LIKE MOM SAID?

OH, COME ON! DO YOU REALLY THINK YOU CAN'T FIND SOMEONE TO LOVE YOU OUT THERE? YOU'RE RIGHT!

Then all of a sudden, I really believed I could make my life better on my own.

Then I second-guessed myself thinking,

HOW WILL I MAKE IT ON MY OWN? CAN I DO IT?

I answered myself:

WELL, YOU'VE BEEN DOING EVERYTHING ON YOUR OWN ANYWAY. OF COURSE YOU CAN DO IT ON YOUR OWN.

I'LL HAVE HALF THE LAUNDRY, HALF THE COOKING, AND HALF THE DISHES. I WON'T HAVE TO JUMP UP TO SERVE COFFEE UNLESS I WANT IT. I THINK I CAN HANDLE THAT.

I chucked weakly, but my amusement quickly faded. I felt sad, mostly for Dick, because I knew I had made up my mind; I was going to tell him I was leaving.

As I pulled into our driveway, I took a deep breath to help collect my thoughts. I was preparing for an emotional night. As I walked into the house and to the kitchen, I saw a card and half-dozen pink roses on the table. I looked at them as if they were aliens wondering what the hell they were for. Then it struck me:

OH YEAH, IT'S YOUR BIRTHDAY. (I was 24.)

My heart sank.

"HOW AM I SUPPOSED TO LEAVE HIM WHEN HE IS FINALLY TRYING?"

Once again, I was a total mess of confusion.

He was upstairs in bed. He was working the graveyard shift and would be getting up for work soon. I climbed the stairs slowly, trying to keep my feelings hidden until I could figure out what I was going to do. The damn flowers had thrown a wrench into my plan.

I got to the bedroom door. "What'd the doctor say?" he blurted out.

I answered, "He said, everything is fine," with such disinterest, he must have noticed.

Without skipping a beat he said, "Good, then let's fuck."

My heart went cold. Any feelings of compassion the card and flowers had evoked were squashed. I turned around without saying a word and went back downstairs.

NOTHING IS EVER GOING TO CHANGE. I JUST HAVE TO FIND THE COURAGE TO SAY, "IT'S OVER. GOOD-BYE."

I went to the kitchen and, again saw the flowers and the card on the table. I almost cried. I was fighting to hold my shattered emotions and the tons of hurt inside. Maybe it was just the straw that broke the camel's back, but all I could think about was the many years of love and caring I'd given to a man who just wants to fuck! Maybe I missed the part where he said, "Did you have a good day?" or "How are you feeling?" Maybe even, "I missed you," or "I love you."

It was getting late so I started to make something to eat before he left for work. I had composed myself by the time Dick came downstairs and I served dinner. I just played with my food most of the time. Finally, he asked, "What's wrong?"

It was impossible to speak with the lump in my throat that had become a hard ache. I would have exploded into tears. Finally, I mustered up enough control to say, "I want to leave. I'm just miserable here." My voice quaked with fear and shattered emotions.

He stood up with his dinner plate in his hand. I ducked my head since David usually threw them, but he went to the trash and slammed the plate into the trashcan.

I started crying uncontrollably. He was angry and hurt, but so was I, and had been for a long time now. He begged and pleaded for me to stay, but I couldn't go on this way anymore. It was destroying me.

The house had a grim air about it for the remainder of the evening. As soon as he left for work, I prepared to leave. I felt hurried, as if I had to get packed and leave quickly. I was afraid he'd come back home to stop me. I was surprised he even went to work.

The fact that I didn't have a job anymore didn't even enter my mind. I didn't know where I was going to stay. I didn't want to go to my mother's; that wasn't a good place to go even when things were going well in my life.

I called Mom to see if I could stay at Oxbrook camp. She didn't mind and told me where she hid the key and I headed out.

I was glad to be there; it was one of my favorite places. I felt a sense of freedom I never felt before. Relieved of all the sadness I had been carrying through too many years of the marriage, but my heart ached for Dick. Then again, my own heart ached for myself. After all, I had spent a good part of my life with this man.

The next morning, I went to see Mom to fill her in on my situation. She'd recently bought a house in Woodland where she rented rooms and asked me if I wanted to stay there and take care of the place. I could live there rent-free. All I had to do was wash the tenants' sheets, keep the rooms cleaned once a week, and collect the rent for her.

Unfortunately, I had plenty of time to spare because I couldn't find a job. It was the mid-eighties and I lived in the poorest county in the state and the poorest state in the Union. The economy was in the tank and there were literally no jobs available. Being desperate, I asked around for work shoveling snow with no success. Several car payments were late and I had a credit card bill to pay, too. I was barely getting by on the $70 a week from unemployment. At least I had a roof over my head and it didn't cost me anything.

With the emotional upheaval in my life, I'd forgotten that I'd filed my income taxes until the check showed up in my mailbox. What a wonderful surprise that was! My refund was only around $600, but it was a small fortune to me at the time.

I knew I needed to get out of the area if I were going to find a decent job. Again, I thought about my father. I wanted to get to Massachusetts to continue my search for him. For a moment, I imagined I might be able to do it.

I COULD STAY WITH FAMILY, SO I JUST NEEDED GAS MONEY TO GET THERE.

I realized it wasn't a bad idea at all. I didn't have a job and I didn't have anything to keep me here—so why not?

Boston was about 400 miles south. It was 1987 and gas was just under a dollar a gallon, so it wouldn't be too expensive to get there. Packing wasn't a problem because I didn't own much more than the clothes on my back.

I was scared. I'd never done anything on my own before let alone look for a father who might completely reject me. Fueling my fear a little more was my mother. She made me promise not to look for him because "I'd ruin his life."

WOULD I? WHAT IF HE WANTS TO SEE ME? ON THE OTHER HAND, WHAT IF HE WISHES I WERE NEVER BORN?

25 - Forty-five Minutes

Between being unemployed and the stress of bill collectors, depression had set in, and I couldn't see any light at the end of the tunnel. Realizing there was no way I was going to get anywhere by staying in Maine, I decided to tell Mom I was going to Massachusetts and look for my father.

Surprisingly, she was okay with it. After telling the family I was leaving, everyone gave me a few bucks to help with the trip. Between the cash gifts and my tax refund, I was in pretty good shape financially. I wanted to leave as soon as possible since hanging around was a waste of time and the money I had.

I went to where it all started with my mother and father, Waltham, Massachusetts, at my Aunt Anna's house. When I told them I was looking for my father, Robert Deacon, my aunt remembered his name, and my cousin Betty vaguely remembered him. The support was very helpful since I was always running into brick walls and resistance for most of my life.

My cousin and I went to some of the local bars and asked a lot of people if they knew Robert Deacon. I was uncomfortable asking all those strangers about someone I didn't even know. It was hard to explain the story, so I pretended he was just an old acquaintance.

After several days of good old fashioned gumshoe detective work, one of the people I talked with told me he thought Robert Deacon worked at a print shop on Lexington Street. It was the first piece of information that gave me a spark of hope.

I went back to my Aunt's, grabbed a phone book, and called every print shop with a Lexington street address asking for Robert Deacon. I'd only made a couple of calls when I got lucky. The voice on the other end of the line said, "I'm sorry; he's not in right now. Can I help you?"

I was stunned and quickly answered, "No. Thank you." I hung up. I was shaking with excitement. My Aunt and my cousin were at work, so I couldn't even share the news. Then I thought:

"NOW WHAT DO I DO?"

Knowing that no one would know who I was, I decided to go to the print shop and see what I could find out on my own. I drove to the address and sat in the car for a minute—I was afraid—not knowing what I was getting into. The building was huge. Inside, there was a sales counter with lots of technical instruments on display. I'd never seen anything like them.

THIS IS NOTHING LIKE MY STEPFATHER'S PRINTING BUSINESS.

A man was behind the counter. We didn't speak other than to acknowledge each other. I noticed some pictures on the wall and thought they might show me something that I could use to help identify my father. I took a closer look. They were various pictures of the owners and employees at parties, events and various other things. I scanned the pictures hoping to see my father's face, although I didn't even know what he looked like.

I kept scanning the pictures and reading the names below them. Then I spotted three well-dressed men who were obviously high-ranking in the company. The caption read: David Deacon, Robert Deacon, and Paul Deacon. I was stunned for a moment. I kept looking from the names to the faces, not believing my eyes. Robert Deacon was not only the president of the company, but he also was in his early sixties.

MY FATHER WOULD BE ABOUT 42 NOW.

My heart sank as I thought:

MAYBE I HAVE THE WRONG FAMILY...

NO... I DON'T THINK SO.

Now I was going on gut feelings and I knew I had to think of all the possibilities, as morbid as they may be.

MAYBE HE'S DEAD.

NO. I DON'T THINK THAT'S IT EITHER.

I kept thinking as my own life flashed before my eyes. I smiled to myself.

MAYBE HE'S THE BLACK SHEEP OF THE FAMILY AND THAT'S WHY HE'S NOT IN THE PICTURE.

I didn't know if I was right, but it felt right—really right. I continued to study the picture a little more. I needed to decide who I was going to call. I picked the man with the kindest, gentlest looking eyes, Paul Deacon.

I went back to my aunt's house to build up the courage to make the call. I figured my father's family owned the company, which wasn't to my advantage. I was afraid they'd assume I wanted something from him or them. All I wanted was my Dad. I didn't care what he had.

None of that mattered right now. I had to figure out how to explain my situation to this man, Paul, without him throwing me out the door. I kept thinking about the phone call I made several years ago when the woman had said. I could be anybody's kid. I still didn't know who she was, and I didn't want to get another reaction like that.

Finally, I picked up the phone and made the call. The receptionist answered again:

Good afternoon, Fotobeam Printing, can I help you?

Me: Hello. Is Paul Deacon in?

Receptionist: Yes. Let me connect you.

Paul: Hello, Paul Deacon speaking.

Me: Hi, my name is Darlene Bickmore. (That was my married name.)

Paul: Yes, how can I help you?

Me: Well, this is about Robert Deacon (now I'm guessing) "Jr."

Paul: Yes?

SO, THERE IS A JR. WHO IS NOT IN THE PICTURE.

Me: It's kind of personal and I'd prefer not to discuss this over the phone.

Paul: Okay, can you meet me in my office in about 45 minutes?

Me: Uh, sure.

Paul: Okay, see you then.

Well, now I'd committed myself and there was no way I was turning back. After waiting for the longest 45 minutes of my life, I drove to Fotobeam to meet with Paul Deacon.

I walked in and waited by the front desk. Less than a minute passed when a man came through a door walking in my direction. I watched him nervously as he approached. My eyesight was never good anyway and I was trying to match his face to the picture. As he got closer, I knew it was him. He introduced himself as Paul Deacon and invited me to his office.

He offered me a cup of coffee. "Yes, thank you," I said and he left the room. I stood there looking at the pictures of his children on a beautiful wooden floor cabinet behind his desk. The similarities were astounding—blonde hair, fair skin, blue eyes, and strong cheek and jawbones. I knew I had the right place.

Paul returned with the coffee. I shook terribly as I took the cup. He noticed my trembling hand and said, "Nothing can be that bad." I chuckled nervously saying, "You wanna bet?"

He sat down behind his desk. "Robert is my brother. What would you like to know?"

I figured I'd just get it out, "Well... I have very good reason to believe that Robert Deacon is my Father." The seconds seemed like minutes as I waited for my little world to come crashing down around me.

"Okay, what would you like me to do?" He said. I looked up at him feeling shock and relief at the same time. It was way too easy.

I stuttered a little and said, "I would like to meet him. I don't want anything from him; I'd just like to know who he is. If he doesn't want me in his life then I want him to tell me. I don't want to hear it from somebody else. I'll never bother him again."

Paul didn't skip a beat and calmly said, "I'm not going to tell you where my brother is, but I will give him your information. He can get back to you if he wants."

"I understand," I said, with personal approval and respect in my voice. "I'd do the same if it were my brother."

I was so happy; I could hardly keep it contained.

"What would you like me to tell him?"

I said, "My mother's name is Jean Fitzgerald. They would have met in Waltham in 1961 around November. I was born in July of 1962 at Waltham Hospital."

I gave him my aunt's phone number and asked him to ask his brother to please call me. Leaving his office, I felt good about what I accomplished. Now, the rest was up to Paul and my father.

Every time the phone rang for the next few days, my heart raced. Finally, the phone rang and this time I held my breath; I somehow sensed it was him. My aunt answered. She nodded letting me know it was him. I started to shake. "Hello, this is Darlene."

"Hello..." (then after a few insignificant pleasantries), he said, "I am so sorry."

I said, "For what?"

"For not being there."

"But, you didn't even know I was conceived, how could you have been there for me?" He was sorry for exactly that reason.

He wanted to meet as soon as possible and, of course, I wanted to meet him. The only catch was he was living in South Florida. I didn't have the money to get there. He didn't have much money either, but said he'd send me a few bucks to help with gas.

Within a couple of days, I got a check for $200 and a note that read: "I can't wait to meet you. Drive carefully. Call if you need anything."

The thoughtful words meant a lot to me. Of course, the money did too. I called him to let him know I got the check. He asked me if I wanted to meet his father, his uncle, and to see Paul again before I left. He said they were looking forward to meeting me. He'd already arranged it with them, so they were expecting to see me before I left the next day.

What I didn't know was one of the first things my father asked Paul was, "Does she look like me?" Without a hint of doubt in his voice, Paul said, "Oh yeah! She's the spit and image of you."

After I arrived, Paul welcomed me as if I were family. As Paul led me through the building, he introduced me to his uncle—the man named "David" in the picture—who worked there too. Everyone, including many of the employees were very nice to me. I wasn't used to this much positive attention.

After spending a little time with my "new" uncle, Paul said, "Now let's go meet your grandfather." We walked silently through the building and stopped in front of a closed door. I looked up at the fancy plaque on the door that read, "President." Paul opened the door and my eyes widened a bit as I entered the huge, elegant office. I quickly looked around at several mounted fish and the head of a white-tailed buck deer mounted on the wall. I felt a little more comfortable as it reminded me of my great grandfather and the hunters back home. The room was very earthy with a lot of beautiful woodwork on the walls.

An attractive man in a nice suit was sitting behind a large wooden desk at the far side of the room. "This is your grandfather, Robert," Paul told me. Robert smiled warmly and said, "Make yourself comfortable," as he gestured to a chair in front of his desk. I tried to hold myself in a posture, to appear proud and poised, but I felt like a pimple on a horse's butt.

I complimented him on the wildlife trophies and told him I came from a long line of hunters and fishermen. Thankfully, my grandfather was quite talkative because I didn't know what to say.

I was glad I'd stopped to see them before I left. This whole adventure was nerve-wracking and one of the scariest things I'd ever done. Although, we had such a positive visit, I now felt a little more comfortable about meeting my father. The one thing I did have was time and the safety of more than 1500 miles to travel before we'd meet face to face.

26 - The Pitter-patter of Big Feet

The following morning, I said my goodbyes to my cousins and aunt and started on my journey to South Florida. As I drove, I felt scared at times and hopeful at times; the combination of feelings came in waves. I kept thinking of how I didn't even know what my father looked like yet; never mind what kind of a person he was. In reality, he was a complete stranger.

As I left hundreds of miles of pavement behind me, I kept delving into my tumultuous life trying to figure out who I really was. It was the first time in my life I could allow myself to be only concerned with me—my true feelings about anything and everything. I always had to consider how Mom would feel first, and then I could feel. I'd learned to do that with everyone. I didn't know people were allowed to think independently. I really didn't know what I liked or disliked, or what I wanted in life.

I allowed myself to feel more anger and resentment toward my mother than I'd ever felt before. I felt hatred for my stepfather and wondered how he could have done the things he did. Then, I thought about Dick and felt the bitterness and pain from years of being taken advantage of, and simply taken for granted.

Anger kept rising and falling in my gut as I thought about how little respect my mother had for me, and how I felt so sorry for her. Then, I felt like a fool remembering how endlessly I'd tried to please her—and had always been there for her—regardless of what she did to me. As I tried to understand

and sort out my rollercoaster feelings plus how I'd felt like such a failure all my life, it struck me…

WHAT IF I'M A DISAPPOINTMENT TO MY FATHER, TOO?"

I was literally frightened by the thought. With no direction and no past to help me prepare for life on my own, I felt so alone. Still, it didn't matter what had happened; it didn't matter who had done what. Right then, what mattered most was me and what I was going to do next.

For just a moment, I stepped outside myself and saw a glimpse of myself from a more objective point of view. I shook my head trying to make that vision go away because I felt pitiful.

I did enough self-analyzing to know I'd been damaged. That's when an anger wave flooded my soul making my head spin. A lot of those waves came and went as I shed rivers of tears on that trip. I realized for the first time in my life, I was broken— a product of the environment I'd grown up in and loathed so deeply.

What I didn't know yet was just how badly I'd been damaged and how much it affected every single thought and everything I did.

It was sometime in the wee hours of the morning when I started to feel tired and knew I had to stop and get some sleep. I stopped and slept in my car near the South Carolina border for about four hours.

The sun blazing through my window and the heat rising quickly in the car woke me up. I rolled down the windows and shook off the sleepiness then started driving again. Stopping for two cups of coffee, I drove until I crossed the Florida state line.

I'VE FINALLY MADE IT!

I was so excited to see that Florida state sign. I kept driving… and driving. Then about four and a half hours later, I thought in my typical backwoods way:

WOW, THIS IS A LONG-ASSED STATE; WORSE THAN DRIVING THROUGH MAINE.

Eventually, I drove into Deerfield Beach. It was about 11 p.m. when I took the exit off I-95.

I knew all the worrying about what he was going to think of me was useless, but I couldn't help feeling uglier and more pathetic as I got closer.

I finally turned down the street where he lived. I studied the address numbers on the houses. They weren't easy to follow because each house number jumped five or more from one house to the next. I kept driving back and forth past the homes within his number range, but I didn't see his.

I narrowed it down to a few houses and turned around one more time to study them closer. I was barely moving down the street when I saw a bearded man in the window of a house. He was watching me quite intently, so I stopped on the street in front of the house.

OH MY! I'VE FINALLY FOUND HIM!

My heart was racing with excitement and fright; I knew it had to be him. Then, he waved his arm to let me know to pull into the driveway. I felt the nervous knot in my stomach tighten. My dream was becoming a reality, but I was so scared.

He came out and stood at the edge of the driveway to greet me. All of a sudden, I felt ashamed. I felt ugly and ruined.

HOW COULD HE BE PROUD OF WHAT HE WAS ABOUT TO SEE?

I put the car in park and froze. I was too afraid to get out. He walked up to my window and said, "Hi." I said "Hi" and we were silent for a moment—a long uncomfortable moment—then he said, "Well, are you going to get out of the car?"

I laughed, trying to hide my nervousness, and got out of the car. We looked at each other for a moment wondering what we were supposed to say or do. I wanted to reach out to hug him, but I was afraid. It was probably just seconds I stood there, but it seemed like forever as an incredible awkwardness came over me. He reached out to give me a hug and I hugged him back tightly; my body went rigid with fright.

We went inside his house and sat in the living room. Neither of us really knew what to say.

"I'm sorry for not having any numbers on the house," he said, "I took them down to paint the house. I've been watching for you since the night before. I'm glad you made it safely."

He told me he was impressed I had the courage to search for him in the first place, and he was happy I was successful in finding him.

He seemed very happy I was there. I suppose that in itself made me feel uncomfortable since I don't remember the last time anyone was happy to see me and he'd just met me.

This was a very frightening time for me. I felt like I still had to—somehow—prove I was his kid; as if I was only a moment from living in the streets if he decided I wasn't his. I was the one who wasn't 100 percent sure he was my father, which isn't surprising since he was the third in a string of my mother's lies.

My awkwardness intensified because he kept staring at me. What I was too nervous and self-absorbed to consider was how he was feeling. He'd just seen his own daughter for the first time.

He stopped staring for a moment and shook his head in amazement. He stood up, "Come here," he said.

Standing up, he took my hand and I followed him across the room to a huge mirror that hung on the wall. I stood beside him looking at the two of us still feeling extremely awkward. "Look!" he said as he pointed at our reflections. He was nearly speechless and I didn't know why.

"You look just like me," he said, as he seemed to beam with amazement and pride. I looked at his face and back at mine to try and see the similarities, but all I could see was a balding, bearded man and an odd-looking girl.

I weakly agreed with him, but I didn't have the heart, or courage, to tell him I just couldn't see it. I remember feeling guilty because I couldn't see what he did.

He said he knew before I got out of the car that I was his child. "Actually," he said, "I had little doubt from the beginning just because of the facts, the timelines, and Paul said you are the spit and image of me."

We sat back down and talked for a while about the long trip and all the details about how I found him. But it was late when I arrived and now it was well after midnight. It had been a long, exhausting trip so he showed me to my room and he carried my suitcase in. We said goodnight and he went to bed.

I smiled as I looked around the room thinking how he'd fixed it up so nicely. It was a good-size room with a double bed and a long dresser under the windows overlooking the back yard. Two big closets took up one wall, which was more space than I needed for my wardrobe.

I got ready for bed and turned out the light. The sounds of night echoed through the house. I'd never been able to sleep well anyway, and I laid there awake; my mind was racing with replays of the evening. As my thoughts slowed, a part of me was half expecting my bedroom door to swing open with him standing there. I tried to tell myself it wasn't even a possibility, but I still couldn't relax. Nothing had ever been normal. Eventually, I fell asleep and didn't hear another thing all night.

The next morning, my father showed me around the house. He had a nice, old Florida-style home with two bedrooms and one bath. The kitchen was small, but ample. Another small room was just off the kitchen toward the back of the house which he used as the laundry room. It also had a door leading out to the back yard. The rest of the house was wide open and the walls were made up of mostly windows within the wall frame. It was like living outside. The palm trees and flowers were beautiful.

He loved to garden. We walked around the yard; he showed me all the tropical trees and plants. Many of them were in bloom with big beautiful flowers in an array of colors. He'd planted a lot of them himself and knew the names of all of them.

Being the only two people in the house, neither one of us had to use each other's name very often. It didn't take long before I realized I didn't know what to call him.

I felt funny calling him "Bob," but a part of me was afraid to call him, "Dad."

"Call me whatever you're comfortable with," he said.

I hated to make decisions. What if my choice wasn't the one he really wanted? I thought the title "Dad" was going to jinx everything I'd hoped and dreamed he'd be. I decided to call him Bob for a while, but it felt stupid and disrespectful, especially since he introduced me to everyone as his daughter with such pride and joy. It wasn't long before I started calling him "Dad."

The next day he wanted to know how I found him. I explained what led me to ask my mother about him in the first place. Then I told him her version of the story. Then, I asked him if he knew I had tried to reach him by phone a couple of years earlier. He closed his eyes for a second and his brow wrinkled as if he was warding off a bad memory. He nodded, opened his eyes, and with a hint of resentment in his voice he said, "It was my mother."

She'd told him about the call and he'd assumed she gotten some information for him; but she'd admitted she'd just hung up on me. He was very upset with her since he had no way of knowing where the call had come from.

He quickly changed the subject and told me he was divorced and never had children. He chuckled and said, "I guess now I'll be hearing the pitter-patter of big feet!" We both laughed; he seemed pleased I shared his sense of humor.

I had only been there a few days and I wanted to find a job; a much-needed job since there was only about $20 left to my name. I told Dad I was going to look for a job. "I think you should just take some time to rest for the next few months and not worry about working."

What he wouldn't tell me at the time is that he knew something was terribly wrong with me. He just didn't know what it was. The more he watched me, the more confused and bewildered he became. All he could do was guess since I wasn't talking. Besides, I didn't know how much the years of abuse had affected me. He thought I might have had an abusive relationship with a boyfriend. He also considered I might have had a learning disability. After all, I didn't speak well and my thick Maine accent made me sound worse. My vocabulary was extremely limited, as were all of my experiences. I hadn't seen much of anything outside of my dysfunctional world.

It was a difficult time for both of us. He hadn't had much experience with children and now he had a 24 year-old daughter with the maturity level of a 10 or 12 year-old. I was an unusual challenge, even for a seasoned parent.

I was clueless as to what was proper, how to dress, or how to conduct myself in public. I didn't know what was proper and acceptable in ordinary society because I'd been living in seclusion most of my life. No one ever taught me anything that mattered.

As we talked and he got to know me a little more, he realized I was very intelligent. As he put it, I had "good survival skills." Although I acted extremely timid, underneath it all he could see I was strong. He'd never seen anything like it and wanted to help me realize and discover my own strengths. My meek exterior was proof I didn't have much faith in myself; he was right about all of it.

Dad still didn't ask any questions or try to pry. I didn't want to say too much about myself as I struggled with my inner turmoil. He figured I'd talk when I was ready.

I desperately needed to feel loved and accepted. I wanted him to be proud of me. I was so damned afraid if he saw how I really felt inside, if he knew everything that had happened in my life, he'd never be able to be proud.

What I didn't know then was that he loved me from the day he saw me. He knew from the moment he laid eyes on me that I was his child.

Not knowing a lot of things, I thought I had to pretend I was something I wasn't. I thought I had to act a certain way and do certain things in order for him to love me. I didn't know how to act or what it was I had to do. I knew how to act back home, but not here; things were different and I didn't know why. I never had to think about it before; I just knew what was expected of me. Now it seemed nothing specific was expected of me and I felt confused.

As the weeks passed, Dad took me everywhere with him. He was kind because he didn't tell me with words, but wanted me to hear other people talk, see how they acted and interacted with each other, hoping I might see it for myself. That's exactly what happened, but it was a painful awakening. I was beginning to notice I was a lot different from other women my age. I didn't fit in at all and I didn't know how to.

Life outside of the isolated world I had known was much different. Besides the rude awakenings about myself, there was a lot of laughter. One of the things I enjoyed most about Dad was his great sense of humor; he made me laugh a lot. I hadn't done much laughing over the years, so it was a complete change from the atmosphere I knew back home. He'd come up with one-liners and wisecracks for just about any occasion and at the most unexpected moments. Laughter really is good medicine.

Fascination set in as I watched other women. I studied how they walked, how they carried themselves, and how they wore makeup. I never had worn makeup in my life. I listened to the way they talked, what their gestures were like, their clothes… everything about them. Before long I felt like an idiot. I knew I stood out like a sore thumb. I didn't carry myself well at all. I didn't know how to wear makeup or how to fix my hair. Even if I dressed in pretty clothes, I felt awkward and clumsy trying to act dainty. I was stiff when I walked and had never worn a pair of heels or nice shoes.

Mom taught me nothing about womanhood and I felt angry. I had become so afraid to act feminine because she'd call me a slut and a whore. I learned to hide it as much as possible.

Meanwhile, Dad didn't know how I was feeling about myself, but he unknowingly made me feel better as he shared his fascination with me and our similarities.

Under normal circumstances, there was a lot about being father and daughter we would have taken for granted. Many of his traits and mannerisms had been duplicated in me simply by genetics; none of them had been learned from constant interaction as in most families with their children. Each time he noticed something new he seemed so proud and happy and I felt more a part of him than before. I needed that confirmation.

He often felt robbed of the chance to see me grow up the way he should have. I was 24 going on 12, and I had a lot of growing up to do for the first time in my life.

27 - Broken in Hidden Places

When Dad went to work, I often played like a little girl. I spent hours in front of the mirror trying to put makeup on. I'd look at myself, sigh with disappointment, wash it off, and try again. Learning how to be a normal woman was going to be a lot of work.

Now that I was able, or should I say allowed-to pay attention to myself for the first time in my life, I saw so many things I didn't like. One of the most unsettling was when I realized how simple, everyday things made me feel terribly anxious. I didn't know how dysfunctional my mother-daughter relationship had been all my life, and I expected the same treatment from my father

For example, one day Dad asked me to go to the grocery store to pick up a few things we needed for dinner that night. Of course, I was delighted since I would jump through hoops for him looking for the approval I needed so much.

I drove a few blocks to the grocery store and went in. Ketchup was on the list so I headed in that direction. There were a lot of choices: squirt bottle, glass, oversized, never mind all the different brand names. I panicked.

I WONDER WHAT HE WANTS.

That was when I realized, I was terribly afraid to make a simple choice let alone the wrong choice. I didn't want him to think I was stupid if I got the wrong kind. So much went through my mind within a minute or less. Feeling ridiculous, I shook my head thinking:

HE'S NOT GOING TO BE UPSET WITH ME NO MATTER WHAT I GET AS LONG AS IT'S KETCHUP.

I grabbed one of the bottles with some lingering apprehension and hoped it was going to be okay. I knew in my heart it was silly, but I couldn't stop feeling afraid. When I got home, I remember waiting and watching for a reaction on how he felt about the ketchup. He helped me unpack the bags. The ketchup wasn't even an issue. I'd worried terribly for nothing.

It was the first time in my life I realized how much fear I felt, or "anxiety" as I chose to call it, since it had always existed in me and now I couldn't admit that I was so very afraid of so many things. The only reason I noticed it at all was because I had nothing to fear. He didn't tell me I was an idiot for not buying his favorite or whatever lame reason my mother could come up with just to be contrary.

Every day I noticed some kind of fear. There was so much it became mind-boggling. I was afraid to get dressed in the morning because I would probably wear the wrong thing and look ridiculous, stupid, or slutty. I was afraid to talk on the phone in front of him in fear I would say something stupid. I was afraid to express my feelings and opinions. I was afraid anytime I had to make a decision on my own because Mom ridiculed me and so often told me I was wrong, stupid, or idiotic.

Sometimes Dad was actually trying to give me good constructive advice and I automatically felt persecuted. All I had to compare his criticism to were my experiences with my mother who always inflicted more harm than good. She didn't offer good advice; just made hurtful comments I call "destructive criticism." Now Dad was trying to help me grow and all I felt was insecure and afraid. I didn't think I was measuring up to his expectations.

He had to handle each unpredictable situation as it arose the best way he could. He couldn't possibly think far enough in advance to figure out what he could do to help make me feel better. He had to wait for me to react with anger or pain to something he'd say or do—that was often purely benign—before he realized I had another problem to deal with. It was confusing for him. "I had to frame my words delicately because I was always afraid of unintentionally hurting your feelings," because that was the last thing he wanted to do. For him, it was like walking on eggshells all the time. Dad was always very direct and to the point with people, but that didn't work with me.

For nearly my entire life, I focused on working hard to earn the love of my mother, and always ended up with her disapproval, anger, violence, or scorn. After that, I felt like a failure and thought I had to work harder to regain her love. Because of that I was convinced my father's love was temporary and it was only a matter of time before I'd screw up and ruin it all by being a disappointment.

If I perceived a hint of what I thought was disapproval, I became terribly afraid. Thinking I was losing his acceptance, which to me meant losing his love. I'd shut down and internalize my hurt and anger.

So many of my fears and painful reactions became obviously unwarranted; they were purely knee-jerk reactions to what was a very real lifetime of abuse. The needless fear was what I noticed most. I had no control over it and that made me feel very broken in hidden places I didn't know how to fix. Over the years Mom had so deeply ingrained fear in me I didn't have time to rationalize; I just reacted like a beaten dog.

I was just beginning to realize my life had never been normal. I'd been abused and it showed. I wanted to tell Dad everything, but again, I was afraid. I was so scared that he'd make me feel as if I was overreacting or being ridiculous the way my mother did every time I expressed my feelings. I thought I might be able to trust him not to hurt me that way. I wanted to burst out with all my sorrows, all my self-pity. I'd be so very vulnerable by exposing my past.

This was going to take courage. Telling my story had always gotten me in trouble. Mom was good at making me out to be the villain or convincing people I was insane. The more I thought about it the more I became afraid, convinced she'd try to make my father think I was lying about everything, and that I was just plain crazy. I knew I couldn't have handled that kind of rejection. My father was my one last thread of hope to make it in this world. I decided to keep my mouth shut.

All my logical thinking conflicted with all my fears, and I wondered why I was so afraid of him. He hadn't given me any reason to feel that way. I was getting so damned tired of feeling afraid and I was becoming angry. I decided I wasn't going to go through the rest of my life feeling afraid. I became convinced it was ridiculous to be afraid all the time and wanted it to stop now, but there wasn't any magical switch and I didn't know how to make it stop.

I knew the source of my problems was hidden in my ugly, shameful past. I also had come to know that there was no way I was going to get over this unless I was willing to face my past all over again; at least to some extent. That would mean talking.

I spent a lot of time thinking. Even when we were watching television, I wasn't paying much attention anymore. I was consumed with my secret turmoil, depression and on the verge of crying. I hated crying in front of anyone, but the lump in my throat was painful and tears began to fill my eyes:

I CAN'T GO ON LIKE THIS ANYMORE. DAMN. I WANT TO DO THIS IN A COMPOSED STATE, BUT I'M ALREADY BEYOND THAT POINT. NOW HE'S GOING TO SEE I'M UPSET AND WANT TO KNOW WHAT'S WRONG.

I couldn't hold it in anymore. I started to cry—silently at first. Then, I quietly blurted out, "I'm so glad I found you."

I kept my head down because I didn't really want him to see me crying. He seemed so happy because he heard the emotion in my voice. "Oh honey, I am too." He reached over for a hug. I quickly hugged him then hid my face on his shoulder and went into a full-fledged—silent—cry.

My voice cracked as I continued, "I've wished since I was a little girl that I knew you. I've cried so many nights, wondering where you could be." I realized it was going to take more than that to make him understand the magnitude of the dread I felt. "Oh Dad, it was awful!"

I started to shake as I finally let go with silent, gut-wrenching sobs. For the first time, I felt sorry for that little girl who just wanted to grow up feeling loved and cared for.

"What was awful?" he asked as he pulled away to look at my face. He put his hands on my shoulders and had to pull back my hair to look at my face. (I always used my long hair to hide my face.) Now, he was very concerned, and that made me cry even more.

What I didn't know was that he'd been waiting for this moment, but what he was about to hear was beyond anything he could have imagined. I was just now realizing how messed up my life really had been. I knew it was hard growing up, but I didn't think too much of that since I'd lived that way all my life. I didn't know anything else until now.

Finally, I composed myself a little and began telling him the story. I didn't tell him everything all at once, but I poured my heart out with a good portion of it. He sat and listened only breaking his silence long enough to ask a question or two along the way.

We cried together for a while. I was afraid to cry aloud, so the tears poured down my cheeks and I just shook. "Let it out, it's okay to cry," Dad said. But I'd forgotten how.

I don't know how long I went on, but I realized I'd been talking and crying for a long time and fear crept in again, so I stopped myself. I didn't want him to get sick of listening to me. I knew I had a lot more to say and I wanted him—I needed him—to listen.

Dad cried saying, "I wish I could have been there for you. All those years, there was nothing I could have done to help you, and your mother is to blame for that!"

At least he had a much better idea of what was wrong with me now. After hearing about my childhood horrors, he wanted to help me get off the heavy barbiturates. I'd been taking them since I was a kid. "I don't think you need them and they're not good for you," he said with determination and certainty.

I had to consider that he could be right. The medication had never stopped the problem. Besides, I hadn't had any trouble with the so-called seizures since I'd moved to Florida.

After considerable thought, I figured it wouldn't hurt to cut my dosage in half for a while. I knew I might have some trouble, but it was worth the try. I also thought the medicine might cause some kind of withdrawal, so I didn't want to stop taking it all at once.

Within a year or so of meeting my father, I'd stopped taking the barbiturates completely and haven't had a problem since. Realizing that I'd taken those drugs since I was 10 or 11—and they never worked other than to keep me in a stupor—made me angry. The "seizures" were most likely a result of the abuse anyway.

I decided to see a neurologist to find out if my suspicions were right. The doctor told me without doing an **Electroencephalography** (EEG), there was no way to be 100 percent sure. After hearing some of my history, he thought it was a very good possibility that the "seizures" were **Psychogenic Non-epileptic Seizures**.

Little by little, I was becoming more aware of how the years of questioning my own sanity had been unwarranted. What I did know was, although I probably wasn't crazy, I was not like most people. What I didn't know was how or what to do to become more like the average young woman and a functional part of society.

In the meantime, like the good little girl I was expected to be, I kept in touch with Mom with a phone call once or twice a week, mostly out of guilt. She usually called me two or three times a week and talked for much longer than I cared to.

The phone rang and I hadn't been paying much attention until I realized Dad was talking to her. I hadn't talked with her since I spilled my guts and hadn't thought to ask him not to tell her I told him all about my wretched life.

Fear gripped me and I looked at Dad with wide eyes as my jaw dropped, wishing I could tell him not to say a word, but he wasn't paying any attention to me.

"Well, Darlene seems very happy to be here," he said. I waited and listened to his side of the conversation, which I could see made him feel awkward just by his demeanor alone.

His conversational tone was becoming more of a firm, matter-of-fact style as he said, "Yeah? Really? Well, she had a pretty rough go of it up there."

He paused. I could only imagine what she was saying to him. "Well I believe her, Jean," he said with a great deal of irritation in his voice. My breathing was shallow, as if I were about to feel her wrath come down on me. His head jerked back slightly and his back straightened as if he were completely surprised. He was silent for about a minute. Then he slowly put the phone back onto the receiver without saying a word. After a few seconds, he turned toward me and shook his head.

"She's crazy," he said with a great deal of conviction. "She hung up on me! I hardly said a word to her and she went off on me."

He sighed with relief; I think. She'd always spoken to him in a bubbly, flirty way. This was the first time he experienced the "other side" of her. I knew it so well, and the evil tongue-lashings that came out of her as if she were slashing me to pieces.

He seemed stunned as he told me about their conversation. "'She yelled at me and said 'She doesn't know what she's talking about; you know she's crazy don't you? She's mental. You can't believe a word she says! She just likes to cause trouble.'"

Now Dad was pissed-off. He said he was repulsed by the horrendous things she was capable of saying about me. He told me he didn't have the heart to tell me everything she had said, but I already had a pretty good idea.

Meanwhile, Dad got more than he bargained for as he watched me go through the many normal things a teenager would. The only difference was, I was learning and struggling through them at the age of 24 while trying to become a healthy, functioning adult.

I began to feel better about myself; at least I thought I was. Often I wore my skirts too short and my clothes too tight and he'd tell me I looked like a slut. That went over like a lead balloon. I felt persecuted all over again. There's no doubt those were harsh words, but he was very blunt sometimes. With my background, that kind of talk seemed normal, but it hurt.

Dad was far from perfect, but he gave me a lot of help and support in many areas. He was smart and always seemed to have some kind of quote or appropriate words of wisdom that helped me grow emotionally.

One of the things I learned about Dad was he didn't really like women very much. He'd been hurt by two divorces, but he was quite the self-admitted playboy and that will kill a marriage fast. His lack of respect and crude comments about women hit me hard. I took them personally when he was often just referring to women in general, but I was a young woman too. All he saw was his daughter struggling to grow up in a troubled childish way. Other times, he saw a young woman. When he went off on a rant about his opinion of women for whatever reason, all I saw was a mean man; much like my mother and so many men I'd grown up around. I'll admit, it set me back a little in my growing process, but it didn't take much after all I'd been through.

The first time I ever walked in a pair of high heels, was not only difficult, it was sadly comical too. Dad shook his head as he watched me go out the door. He thought I looked like a little girl wearing her mother's shoes for the first time.

For a long time, I bought clothes and dressed for the simple purpose of trying to appear sexy. I'd never been allowed to dress like a woman or look remotely sexy before. I thought it was great. When it came to attracting men and feeling loved, my self-image was hinged upon how well I could attract the opposite sex. It took me a few mistakes before realizing I was attracting men who only wanted one thing—the only thing I thought gave me value—sex.

28 - Going Back to Maine

Meanwhile, I think the poignant conversation— in addition to several that followed—piqued Dad's interest in meeting her in person.

Besides, I wanted him to see where I grew up. It was such a beautiful part of the country. We talked about it and made plans to drive up since it was more affordable in those days.

I was very nervous about going back to Maine. I'd heard that Mom and David had quit drinking about a year before—that made me feel a little better about the trip—but I wondered what they'd be like. Another part of me wondered if they really had quit or if they'd just made another failed attempt and were hiding it.

We took turns driving to New England in four-hour shifts. We arrived in Massachusetts after about 24 hours and stopped at a motel to rest.

After stopping, I had some time to think about seeing my mother again. Obviously, the memories were not pleasant and that's when I realized I wasn't really looking forward to it. I started to get scared. It had been so long since I'd seen my mother sober, I didn't know what to expect. Then deep fear set in; I didn't know what I was so afraid of and started to cry. Then I said, "Dad, please don't leave me up there, no matter what happens."

He hugged me and told me he'd never do that. I didn't know why I was so frightened. A part of me was afraid Mom would convince him I was so insane; he'd leave me there. I knew she was capable of doing just about anything and I always ended up on the losing end.

Meanwhile, I hadn't thought about what Dad was thinking. I was too wrapped up in my own terror to consider him. I did that a lot back then. "I'm very curious to meet the monster who raised you," he said. I could see that he was still pissed off at her, but he also knew there was no sense in starting trouble that I'd probably pay for anyway. He said he'd approach her as if they were starting from level one.

After driving up the entire Eastern Seaboard, we both breathed a sigh of relief as we pulled into Mom's driveway. We were quiet as we walked up to the door. I knocked politely and we waited. My mother answered and welcomed us both inside.

The greeting was uncomfortable for me; I felt like a stranger to them. A lot was going through my mind, like how David was going to handle my father's presence. His jealousy would normally make this visit impossible. I had visions of Mom embarrassing me with some unwarranted, flirtatious actions.

Nonetheless, everything went smoothly and we all sat down to talk at the kitchen table. This was an interesting time for my father, too. After all, he was sitting in front of the woman he'd slept with 25 years ago and I was the result of that short affair.

The same woman who had flipped out on the phone with him like a raving lunatic trying to convince him I was a liar, insane and liked to cause trouble, was putting on a great act of perfection; maybe too good. She acted conspicuously normal, flawless, and fake. She didn't show any signs of weakness or human error. She hid it all so well, as if nothing had ever happened which convinced him she was a master of deception and, as he said, a cunning, wicked woman.

Dad figured she was either trying to prove I had lied about everything, or she was afraid to do anything that might piss him off. She knew he wouldn't allow her to hurt me again.

He told me later, "I could tell by the look in her eyes, she knew she was powerless over you now."

I didn't see it because the truth was; I was still giving her the power to control my fears. But, there was a level of confidence in me and it was beginning to show. I suppose it was because Dad was there with me and I knew I was safe. Confidence was a characteristic my mother had never seen in me before.

With all the horrors I'd told him about my childhood, he felt more driven to analyze and try to find out what my mother was really like so he could form a conclusion of his own. Ultimately he thought, "As much as I wanted to be here for Darlene when she was growing up, I'm glad I wasn't with HER."

The next day, Mom decided we should head out to Oxbrook camp. Aunt Jo and Uncle Tony now owned it, but they rarely had time to use it. I thought it was a great idea since I'd always loved it there and I couldn't wait to show Dad. I was excited as I told him we were going to camp. "Camp! Where's camp?" he asked.

I told him it was in the middle of the woods. "I thought we were already in the middle of the woods!" he said with a bit of shock in his voice.

"This is civilization to the people here; camp is in the woods."

Dad couldn't get over how far into the forests of Maine we were and he felt sorry I had to grow up there, although he couldn't deny that the wilderness was gorgeous. I told Dad for me it was peaceful to be able to walk in the woods. The beauty of nature was the one thing I could depend on and enjoy. No one could ruin it for me. No one bothered me when I was alone in the woods and it was about the only peace I could find.

Dad and I also visited with my grandparents, and Aunt Jo and Uncle Tony. My mother and David didn't seem to want to have any part of the family gathering, so they stayed at camp.

We'd had a good time and had been in Maine for about five days now. Dad was getting bored and he was looking forward to visiting with his family in Massachusetts.

After we got home, I took a good look at myself and realized I had a lot of work to do… on myself. I focused on my past and rehashed a lot of it with Dad. Somehow I knew the answers to most all of my problems were there; in my dark past full of abuse that I'd learned I had to keep secret.

After talking with Dad one night, I said, "Sheesh! I ought to write a book."

It was more of an off-the-cuff comment than anything.

"Why don't you?" he said with a deep and real emphasis.

I just looked at him with surprise; realizing he was serious. I tossed the idea around in my head for a minute. I was actually considering it. Back then, I don't think either of us thought I'd finish the book.

I didn't realize what I was getting myself into—this wasn't just about writing events—it became a thorough examination of those events and the effect they had on me. I had to dig deep into myself and I found places and things about me that I didn't like at all. I knew if I were going to heal and learn to correct the years of "bad programming" that had become second nature, I had to analyze myself with severe scrutiny. Then I was forced to face everything about myself whether I liked it or not—if I were going to correct that bad programming.

In the short time I'd lived with my father, I realized that fear was my emotional ball and chain. I was impatient for a cure and extremely frustrated because I couldn't find one. Of course, I hated feeling afraid all the time. What's worse was I knew in my mind that there was little to no reason for me to feel that way, but I couldn't control it. My fears had consumed me physically and mentally. Anytime I felt fear creeping in, I couldn't concentrate on anything beyond the moment. I was so afraid of daily life, and its everyday encounters with challenges and simple decisions, that I'd shut down and do nothing.

For no reason other than my own insecurities and my past to use as a guide, I was afraid of my father emotionally. Always afraid I'd never measure-up to his standards, the same way I had consistently failed to measure-up to my mother's expectations. I still couldn't shake the fear of disappointing him and I was convinced if I did he wouldn't love me and wouldn't want me around anymore.

Mom's anger had been such a consistent part of my life; I began to take it upon myself to try to make her happy. Now I was doing the same thing with my father. Throughout my entire childhood, I relentlessly tried altering my thoughts and actions to win my mother's love, support, and encouragement. I failed on every front. Now, I still thought it was my duty to "earn" these things.

All children need their parents to show them love. That didn't exist for me. I was often heartbroken because so many things I thought I'd done so well my mother reduced to barely acceptable, or not acceptable at all. Mom always showed a negative reaction or simple lack of interest. Ultimately, I'd learned that my very best was insufficient and kept blaming myself for the failures when there really was no way to win. Eventually, my **self-esteem** was practically non-existent and I believed I was completely incapable of doing what was necessary to be loved and cared for.

The desperate need I had to please my mother went so much deeper than the fear of failure. As children, our parents are our lifeline. Without them we can't survive and, although we may never think of that consciously, we inherently know it. That fear is part of why I never stopped trying to win her approval. I believed if I were to fail so badly, she'd hate me and abandon me, and then I might die—no mother, no life.

"Conditional love" was a term I'd never heard before reading a multitude of self-help books, but I'd lived under it all my life. As a child, I had to earn my love. Dad told me his love was not dependent upon whether or not my actions, my thoughts, or my anything agreed with his or even met his expectations.

I'd never felt comfortable being myself around anyone; I'm not sure I knew what being myself was like. I'd always acted the way I thought others wanted me to act or said what I thought they wanted to hear. I was a people pleaser, which made me a manipulative liar and I didn't even know it. I thought I was being a "nice" person. In reality, I was being deceitful in an attempt to avoid conflict.

I also realized I didn't know how I felt about most things either because I'd always stifled my own feelings and pretended to feel the same way my mother did so I'd be in total agreement with her. If I expressed an opposing opinion or showed feelings that weren't in line with hers, I risked further scorn for being ridiculous and wrong.

These behaviors are a result of the co-dependency I referred to earlier, and I had a severe case of it. Sometimes I reacted with the **Fight or Flight Response** that animals display. For example, if you were to frighten a cat, even unintentionally, its reaction will be to attack or run. Conversely, most humans have the ability to think intelligently and analyze those situations that cause us to feel afraid or threatened. I didn't have that ability.

As a child with no life experience, I analyzed whatever it was that caused my mother's anger, or the action that created fear within me, and then I reacted the best way I knew to protect myself emotionally or physically. In other words, when my mother became angry, instead of biting her or running because I felt frightened, I took it upon myself to buffer the anger she took out on me. Whatever it took, and no matter how I felt, I'd try to take control of the situation in an attempt to alter my mother's anger to protect myself. Those reactions became natural, so to speak, and were often illogical and ineffective, but so was my situation. There was no doubt I was an **Adult Child of an Alcoholic**. Now those reactions weren't necessary, and I was beginning to notice my own dysfunctional behavior.

I usually burdened myself with the blame for everyone's unhappiness. I can see now I never had that much influence over anyone. I never had any control over their happiness or misery. As a co-dependent child and now an adult, I wanted everyone to be happy, and if they weren't, I tried in vain to make them feel that way.

I actually caught myself using the Fight or Flight Response one day. It was good that I was able to recognize what I was doing, but it was also upsetting when I realized I'd been like that all my life.

Dad's cousin was visiting. She was doing something and raised her voice in frustration. I sensed the tension building and got nervous. Whatever happened had nothing to do with me, and I had no reason to try to protect myself from her anger. Still I felt afraid and, without thinking, I got up and started cleaning the kitchen. There was nothing I could do to make the situation better for her. I reacted by doing something helpful and positive in an attempt to avoid becoming the target of her anger.

That was the first time I consciously realized what I was doing and why.

WHAT AM I DOING? I'VE BEEN DOING THIS ALL MY LIFE! HER ANGER HAS NOTHING TO DO WITH ME ... IT'S OKAY IF SHE'S ANGRY ... IT'S NOT MY FAULT ... SHE'S NOT GOING TO GET MAD AT ME JUST BECAUSE I'M STANDING HERE ... SHE'S NOT MY MOTHER.

I had to think it through logically before I was able to talk myself into relaxing with the situation. I'd finally realized there was no logical reason for me to act that way anymore, but then again, there was no logic in the way my mother redirected her anger onto me either—I simply didn't know any better—until now. No one around me was taking their anger out on me. The actions I once took to help keep myself safe for so many years were now unnecessary and, thankfully, that was becoming obvious to me.

Unlearning my dysfunctional behaviors was going to be the most difficult part of my recovery. It's a lot harder to unlearn something than it is to learn it right the first time with no prior bad habits. Here's an example of one thing I had to unlearn:

It may seem obvious to some, but Dad had to teach me that opinions are just someone's interpretation of a situation or thing. If I shared my opinions with my mother, she usually made me feel as if I were stupid or wrong if they disagreed with hers. She was verbally brutal about it. I learned to keep my thoughts to myself and just agree with her at all times.

"Opinions are neither right nor wrong; they just are. So, if your opinion of something differs considerably from someone else's, that's neither wrong nor right, that's just the way it is," Dad said. That struck home with me and made so much sense I had to wonder why I didn't figure it out on my own.

For many years I battled with the fear of doing anything that took initiative because I was convinced I'd fail. I was afraid to express my own feelings and opinions because I knew I'd be wrong. I couldn't make a choice, even a simple choice, without the fear of feeling stupid or ridiculous again.

My life had improved greatly and, because of that, there were days when I felt like I was on top of the world and other days when I felt completely dejected.

Dad kept drilling the same messages into my head to help me believe them myself. He kept telling me I never did anything wrong, and I always did a good job with the things I did. He told me I didn't need to worry about making mistakes; everyone makes them, and it's okay.

I believed him, but that feeling of anxiety wasn't going to go away easily. My fears had subsided somewhat and I didn't feel as anxious over every little thing anymore. There were times when I was overwhelmed with pure panic. I couldn't control my breathing, and it felt like I was running out of oxygen. After all the things I'd been through, fear was the one thing I couldn't get a handle on. I knew it was the core of a majority of my problems.

I knew in my logical mind I didn't have to feel that way, but uncontrollable emotions wouldn't let me stop. Dad told me just because there didn't seem to be an immediate reason for me to feel afraid, didn't make my fear any less real.

It was so confusing to me. Somehow, he made sense of what seemed senseless. I often thought I was beyond repair. I was simply tired of feeling afraid of such stupid little things the average person could never understand. I know now I wasn't alone. I see the same kind of fear in other people today, but at the time I felt very alone and very foolish.

Another thing that had become very important to me was to try to understand why my mother treated me the way she did. I always thought it was pure hatred toward me. I believed I needed to forgive her to some degree in order to help heal myself.

One thing that helped me greatly over the years was when Dad said, "Anger is always a result of hurt." It applies to so much of my story, to me, and life in general. Those seven words made an enormous difference in my perspective on my life and my reactions to so many things.

Over the course of my self-help studies, I've added "fear" and "guilt" to that seven-word phrase. I did that because fear was the deepest reason for most of my anger. The fear of abandonment was at the top of the list. I was afraid my father would discard me if I disappointed him enough. That's when I realized that the one person who could hurt me the most at this point in my life was my father. I was afraid of losing his acceptance more than anyone else's. It was my problem, not his. I felt the horrible fear of my mother's scorn and disapproval return anytime I disappointed him, or even perceived that I'd disappointed him. Sometimes I assumed I'd disappointed him simply because I interpreted his reaction or response incorrectly.

This is when my ability to be honest with myself made an enormous difference. It was painful to admit that my feelings of fear and anger were a result of such a horrible deficiency within myself. It was my inability to differentiate between real and perceived personal attacks. What's more, I didn't know how to handle either one.

As I slowly gained some self-esteem and confidence, I also began to realize, I'd been reacting instinctively as a means of protection from the pain or fear I felt, not because of what someone had said or done.

Dad had a library of little quips and sayings that just popped out of his mouth whenever I needed them the most. He never pushed anything on me or tried to convince me to think the way he did. He gave me these little verbal tools for me to use as I wished. Sometimes I didn't understand them at the time, but when the right circumstances presented themselves, one of his little sayings would pop into my mind and it would finally make sense.

He told me that most things people say and do were not meant to hurt me and I had to stop acting as if I were still a victim.

I'M NOT A VICTIM!

At least, I didn't want to think I was. The reality was; I'd been terribly victimized. The point he was trying to make is that I didn't have to act like a victim anymore. He was right, and that was another big leap toward becoming well. I realized I'd come to believe I deserved to be the target of everyone's anger because I didn't have to be doing anything wrong for Mom to spit in my face or slap me; she just had to be angry. I believed and acted as if it was my responsibility to make sure everyone was happy. If they weren't, then somehow I'd failed; it was my fault.

There were so few times in my life when I could listen to my gut feelings and actually follow them. I'd become accustomed to acting upon my fears and not listening to my inner voice; the same voice that so often protects us or guides us along the right path. Now I had the opportunity to make choices based upon how I really felt, not how someone else felt. A lot of what Dad was trying to teach me was beginning to make sense. I was starting to feel as if I had a better handle on my own emotions. I no longer had to let my emotions rule my actions.

I gained a little more faith in myself and started listening to what my **conscience** was telling me. I hadn't been able to do that in years.

I believe the feelings derived from our conscience is God (or part of my perception of God). Hopefully each one of us is given a conscience at conception. We can do what is right by identifying those feelings triggered by our conscience.

I didn't understand the power of a conscience back then. I called it my gut feelings and they were telling me that my life was very wrong and so were the people in it. But I had a hard time believing something so intangible in a world that was so ugly and real. It was a powerful feeling and I have to assume it came from something outside myself that I was unable to fully understand.

29 - Stepping Beyond the Disrepair

I do believe the human conscience will invoke feelings that are pertinent to whatever is happening at the time. My conscious tells me a lot just by the way it makes me feel before I'm about to do or say something. It may be good, bad, exciting, or even frightening, but it will have a message. The emotion I feel is a good indicator of whether or not my actions will be right or wrong. However, that feeling may or may not agree with what I want to do, but I believe it will guide me to do the right thing. In other words, my conscious is my judge.

Now, that doesn't always mean I interpreted those feelings correctly. For instance, if my intention were to steal something, my conscience would create a feeling of fear and nervousness because I know stealing is wrong. On the other hand, there was a time in my life when I would have felt excited by the thought.

This is where some people may learn to interpret those conscience based feelings incorrectly and, if unchecked, may do so for the rest of their lives.

When I was a child my mother had not only asked me to steal for her, but she was pleased when I did it for her. I'd learned that, although stealing is illegal, my mother would be proud of me for doing it, and I would have done anything to make Mom happy. Obviously, my values were warped and my conscience was only as good as the values I was taught.

Still, I often found myself too afraid to listen to my conscience. What it was telling me usually meant I had to do something emotionally frightening to achieve a given result. That action may have been to correct myself in some way or to make a serious change in my life to improve my own behavior. It didn't mean the feeling was wrong; it just meant it would take a lot of courage and good use of my common sense to work through.

When I felt angry about something, I had to remember that I only felt angry because I was hurt, afraid or felt guilty for some real or perceived reason. Once I was able to admit that I'd been hurt, felt afraid, or guilty, then I was able to handle the situation with intelligence and, more appropriately, without allowing the anger to mask the pain and fear.

Once I started to honestly acknowledge my thoughts, feelings, and emotions, I could also share them with my father. It brought about a new level of communication. We could deal with problems as they arose instead of dealing with the aftermath of my anger and illogical reactions.

I came to the conclusion that when I felt anger or fear creeping in, I had to stop and take a moment to force my emotional reaction aside. This wasn't easy since I'd been doing this without thought for as long as I can remember; it was instinctual, not logical.

This is when I realized that there was a difference in the terms I used: "respond" versus "react." I'd been reacting the way an animal does—by instinct and emotion alone—the flight or fight response. I learned that I did have the ability to reason and think rationally to achieve a logical and peaceful conclusion.

It wasn't long before I realized that Dad was right; most often what he'd said or done wasn't meant to hurt me at all. I'm using Dad as an example since I was overly sensitive to him more than I was to anyone else simply because I thought I had to win his approval constantly.

On the other hand, if I honestly felt a person's intent was to hurt me, then I had to re-evaluate the reasons I was tolerating such behavior.

Now, at the age of 50, and with so many more years of my mother's not-so-loving words and actions, I've determined that she really was a hurtful person. I've watched her do it to a lot of people, so it isn't just me and it never was. Aunt Jo and I have talked about it at great length. She knows first-hand since she's been a victim of her sister's cruelty since they were children.

Out of a desperate need to understand how my mother could have treated anyone—never mind her own daughter—the way she did, I was driven to research my own mother. From my studies, as a non-professional, I've learned that my mother is **Narcissistic with Sociopathic Tendencies** also known as **Narcissistic Personality Disorder and Borderline Personality Disorder** for the more politically correct. Now, I truly don't believe she could stop her brutally destructive behaviors.

I was growing and healing, but I'd gotten to a point where I was feeling stifled. I could depend on my father to confirm my thoughts and feelings, which I needed at the time because I didn't know how to feel or think on my own.

I'd successfully faked my way into a good job with little to no experience, so I was perfectly capable of taking care of myself financially, but I still couldn't take care of myself emotionally. I often drove Dad nuts by trying to act out my co-dependent behaviors and there seemed to be nothing he could do to make me stop. This was one thing I had to do on my own, so I had a big problem. I didn't realize how co-dependent I still was and how it affected nearly every facet of my life.

My gut was telling me it was time to live on my own. It only seemed logical that I'd gain my emotional independence with practice. That would mean thinking, feeling, and living without anyone else's influence, including Dad's.

I didn't realize I was afraid of being alone. I'd never been alone long enough to be myself, and I don't think I knew who I was anyway. I thought I needed to have someone to love me to feel worthy.

So, instead of facing the fear of being alone, I met a man named Warden. I thought I fell in love and moved in with him. Maybe I did love him and maybe he loved me, but it was for all the wrong reasons on both our parts. Obviously, I'll only address mine.

He was six feet eight inches tall, handsome, and reminded me a lot of Paul Bunyan. He was very gentle and seemed kind. He'd just gotten divorced and had a four-year-old son.

What I was really doing was running away. Avoiding the work I needed to do on myself.

Eventually, I was supporting both of us while he sat home all day. He was miserable with his life and, I assume, with himself.

I'd come home from work and he'd be stoned and sitting on the couch while his four-year-old son sat around waiting for someone to pay attention to him. The situation became pitiful and I'd allowed it.

I finally began to feel like a fool, realizing I'd been assuming the blame for his unhappiness. He wouldn't share his obvious feelings of sadness with me, but he allowed me to feel and act as if it were my fault. I felt lonelier than if I'd been living alone. It took a while, but I finally realized there was nothing I could do to make him feel better. He didn't seem to care about anything anymore—especially me. I decided to go "fishing" and said, "You know, if I were to fall off the face of the earth tomorrow, I don't think you'd give a damn."

I was fishing for some kind of response that might show me he felt something—anything—but, as usual, he said nothing; not a damn word. I stood there stunned and broken-hearted. I knew it was time for me to leave.

I moved back home with Dad. He wasn't very happy about me moving in with this guy in the first place, but the one thing he didn't want to do was control my decisions. Dad knew I was better off going through a few growing pains and learning something valuable in the process.

I'd definitely grown up a lot through this experience. I have to admit that I was proud of myself because I found the courage to leave the unhealthy relationship. In the past, I'd have clung to him like a vine to a cold, damp, stone wall and kept trying to make it all better.

The most valuable lesson I learned was no matter how much effort I put into trying to make him happy, it wasn't going to happen. I couldn't change the way he felt about me, or himself, or anything else for that matter.

Dad had yet another little saying and it applied to this situation. I didn't completely understand it for quite some time. I often didn't understand his little lessons right away. I was so severely blinded by years of doing everything the wrong way, I didn't know there were other options.

Dad recited the "Serenity Prayer:"

GOD GRANT ME THE SERENITY TO ACCEPT

THE THINGS I CANNOT CHANGE,

COURAGE TO CHANGE THE THINGS I CAN,

AND THE WISDOM TO KNOW THE DIFFERENCE.

"God grant me the serenity to accept the things I cannot change.

OKAY; SOMETIMES I CAN'T CHANGE THE WAY THINGS ARE.

"Courage to change the things I can."

I NEED TO FIND THE COURAGE TO CHANGE THOSE THINGS I KNOW I CAN.

"And the wisdom to know the difference"

I needed to recognize when I was able to make changes, and to know when I had to accept reality and not try to make or force changes.

I still had a lot of mending to do. I was unhappy with myself and I kept searching for a way to fulfill the emptiness I felt inside myself. I didn't realize I was doing exactly what Mom had done all her life; I was trying to fill a void inside myself with someone else's love. That void was only my own lack of self-esteem, self-confidence, and love. I had not yet learned there was no way of filling that void until I learned to love myself.

I knew at this point, I needed to be on my own—by myself—alone. In reality, I wasn't going anywhere in a hurry; I was still emotionally afraid to be on my own.

Dad agreed and said being alone would be easier than getting myself into another relationship anyway. He was right. So far, my relationships had been difficult and unhealthy.

I was about 26 and I'd finally landed a full-time job as a corporate secretary, so money wasn't the issue; my insecurity was the issue. Each time I saw something about myself that was broken I went to the library or a self-help bookstore and studied. I'd read and re-read until the messages and lessons sunk in. Sometimes it took months for me to understand the simplest of things in these books. These were deep-seated issues within me.

I decided to take the leap and began to look for an apartment—by myself. Then I realized I was scared. I told Dad how I felt and said it even sounded silly to me. He was reassuring and told me he'd always be there for me. "Some psychologists say one of man's biggest fears is the fear of being alone," he said. That made me feel a little more "normal," but I knew I had to face this fear head-on. It prevented me from overcoming a part of that co-dependency which was hindering so much of my growth.

Fear had been such a huge part of my everyday life and I had a hard time determining when it was normal to feel scared. I had gotten to the point where I thought it was wrong to feel scared at all. The truth is, everybody feels scared sometimes—it's normal, but what isn't normal is when I let those fears stop me from growing or doing or just being me.

Now I had to step beyond my **comfort zone**, which at that time was a very small place. In the past, if I found myself in a position where I had to do or say something that made me uneasy, I tried to avoid the situation or confrontation completely because I risked putting myself in a vulnerable position. By learning to step beyond my comfort zones, intelligently and with the guidance of my conscience, I usually gained a valuable growing experience.

This crude graphic is what I call my "Cylinder Pyramid". Imagine that "comfort zones" are cylinders, infinite numbers of them, starting with the tallest and most narrow one in the center.

Each cylinder that surrounds the next also becomes shorter and wider as they go outward.

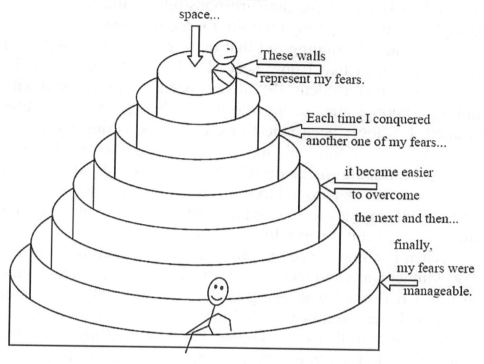

A good example of how I allowed my fears to keep me within my comfort zones is the years I spent with my husband. Even though it may have been unhappy and unhealthy, it was easier to face a daily life of discontentment than to do something about it. There were a couple of reasons for that. One of them was because the life was familiar to me and I knew what to expect from it. Another reason was that I was afraid to tell him because I knew he'd be upset. My fear-driven codependency wouldn't allow me to put myself in a position to be the target of his anger or feel guilty for hurting him with the truth. Also, that horrid "fear of the unknown" kept me right where I was. I didn't think I had the courage to deal with the outside world, thinking it may be worse than the situation I was in at the time.

Making any drastic change in my life was frightening. I decided to take a fearful leap and get a place of my own. I'm not about to tell you that living alone wasn't a bit scary at first, but I also felt a sense of freedom, responsibility, and most of all, complete control over my own life for the first time.

I was quickly finding out that there were a lot of skills I'd never developed that I now needed. I had to learn how to be emotionally independent. I'd always been so preoccupied with doing, thinking, and feeling the way I thought everyone else wanted, I'd never been able to experience anything the way I really felt. I was too busy looking at everyone else's feelings instead of looking inside myself. Now, I was truly alone and I didn't have anyone around to think about before I did anything. My actions, my desires, my wants and needs were all based on me and how I felt. I was a little lost at first.

When I started to see over the walls of my comfort zones—my cylinder walls and fears—and what I believed were my limits in life, I realized I was living in the very tiny, but tall, center cylinder. I was afraid of everything outside those walls of my cylinder. Within that tiny cylinder I had limited myself to the amount of life I could enjoy, the people I would meet, the joys and learning I should have exposed myself to, but I was too afraid of the unknown life outside my "safe" walls. By staying behind those walls, I would only experience a small fraction of what the world had to offer.

I wanted to meet new people and make new friends. There was so much to do, but I was afraid.

WHAT IF I MAKE A FOOL OF MYSELF? WHAT IF I FAIL? WHAT IF I REALLY CAN'T MAKE IT "OUT THERE"? WHAT IF "THEY"—THE ALMIGHTY GENERAL POPULOUS—SEES HOW INEXPERIENCED I AM? WHAT IF THEY NOTICE HOW FRAGILE AND AFRAID I REALLY AM?

Then, from somewhere inside, I felt the pain of realizing I had just described myself as a fool, a failure, ignorant, and scared out of my own wits. That little voice inside was telling me I had to keep facing each fear head-on. Each cylinder wall—each fear—that I overcame helped me live life a little more. I had to risk being seen as human and not feel as if I were weak or stupid for being so human.

As I conquered the walls of each comfort zone, the next one was easier. Each time I was able to overcome another fear, the next one seemed so much smaller, and the walls of my cylinders—my fears—kept getting shorter, or smaller.

I didn't go out and start making friends and greeting the world with open arms, but I did take baby steps. I started saying hello and striking up conversations with my neighbors and co-workers. Before now, I'd only do the minimum and say a quick "hi" on the way by, but never stopped to chat or share any thoughts. I was afraid to risk sounding stupid or having an idiotic idea.

I began to realize the only person I really had to impress was myself (providing my thought process wasn't skewed.) I had begun to make decisions based on facts and what my little voice inside was telling me instead of making those decisions and choices based on what someone else may think of me because of my decision. I could now see that by listening to and following the voice of my conscience I was making good decisions and choices. The more I saw myself doing the right thing and feeling good about myself, the more people I attracted who had the same good qualities. As they say, "Birds of a feather flock together."

Still, I had a lot of growing to do. I could still see I was holding back a lot because of my lingering fears. I didn't have the same level of confidence I saw in other women, so I watched and tried to learn from the people I admired the most.

I found that the hardest part of living alone and not having a steady boyfriend was feeling unloved. I still felt as if I needed someone to feed me all that love and affection I'd missed all my life. Deep down, I knew no one should be so needy. I knew in my heart I still didn't feel worthy enough on my own and I had to reach that point somehow. I realized I had to learn to be content and fulfilled on my own or I'd never be capable of having a healthy relationship.

For a long time, I hated the saying, "If you don't love yourself, then you can't love somebody else." That just sounded so self-centered to me, but it wasn't. Now I was beginning to understand why my lack of love for myself was getting in the way of everything I wanted to achieve.

I didn't want to make the same mistakes my mother had all her life by trying to fill the empty feeling she felt inside with something or someone else. Although my mother was a very bad example to follow, I learned a lot from it.

As I began to grow and change, sometimes I'd outgrow the people I'd become close to and that was hard. I'd always been quick to fall in love—probably because I was so needy. Now I was learning that having someone to love me didn't make me worthy. It just helped distract me from my personal emptiness... temporarily. It also gave me another reason to avoid dealing with myself, my feelings, my deficits, and other personal problems. Those were the things I had to address and would one day bring me to a place where I'd find myself worthy. My attention was drawn to them and away from myself.

That empty feeling was horrible and I'd allowed it to influence the way I listened to my little voice inside. I needed to feel loved so much that I ignored compatibility, alcoholism, and even abuse in a relationship. The pain and fear of abandonment were often so great, I chose not to listen to my conscience telling me that something was wrong.

Again, I could hear Dad say, "Give yourself a chance." I didn't like it though. I was lonely. I reviewed all my previous relationships and how they'd always ended up failing. Not only had I been cheating myself, but I had also deceived the other person by letting them believe they were everything I ever wanted in a mate. The day always came when I realized that the hollow feeling inside of me I thought I'd filled was still empty. It was a lot of work for too much unhappiness and hurt feelings; I couldn't do that to myself again.

That led me to another awakening. I had to be able to accept people for who they were, not who I wanted them to be. Instead of choosing to try to change someone—something I now know is impossible to do—I had to accept them for who they were.

Dad told me time and time again, "It's not your job to change others nor is it your job to make everything around you perfect. People aren't perfect and the world is not a perfect place."

It finally sunk in. I had to consider myself first. Anytime I'd put the needs of others, or what I thought were their needs, ahead of myself I was only neglecting me. Inevitably, I'd eventually become resentful of the person I was with. I'd blame them for my feelings of neglect. Sometimes I'd feel used or taken advantage of. Occasionally I'd think of how much I did for them with little in return. The truth was, if I hadn't ignored my feelings, wants, and needs in the first place, I most likely wouldn't have ended up in the situation at all.

"Communication is the key to everything," Dad would tell me. I've taken that phrase very seriously since then. Half-truths and missing information are another way of not communicating properly. I did it for years by not expressing my feelings, or myself, especially when I was hurt. I can't expect anyone to read my mind or know how I'm feeling, so I learned to address situations in my personal and, when appropriate, my professional life as they arose instead of waiting or not doing it at all.

If all the cards are on the table, then everyone involved has a better chance of achieving positive results in everything they do. When we work with bad information or lies, then we're wasting time working on something that isn't even real; and reality—or the truth—nearly always becomes known by all.

For a long time, it scared me to share my vulnerabilities with other people. That was part of what kept me from asking for help. I've made close friends with people by asking for advice or help with something. I was afraid of women for years, but with a mother like mine that's understandable. Now, I wouldn't want my life to be without good female friends. I can share my most vulnerable moments with them only. It is nice to find out I'm only being human and they were feeling very similarly about sine of the same things themselves. That vulnerability often brings people closer and we develop close relationships. Trust is important in this, though. That can be hard since trust is the one thing that was ripped to shreds as a victim of child abuse. Give time and good examination to your friends to determine if they are trustworthy. The one thing that helped me, and still does in so much that I do, was listening to my inner voice... really listening. Wait for it.

I had a lot to overcome since I left Maine. There were times when I still got angry with my mother and stepfather for what they'd done to me. I guess I had to get angry with them in order to forgive myself, but there came a time when anger was no longer productive. I had to direct my energy to where it would be the most beneficial, and that was to help myself. No amount of finger pointing and blaming was going to help me get over the traumas and correct my dysfunctional behaviors. There was only one person responsible for how I was going to ultimately turnout; that was me.

Anytime I was faced with another difficult challenge in my personal growth that I couldn't seem to overcome, I'd hear myself say, "I'm trying."

Even the definition of "try" is "attempt." It wasn't until I was in a therapy session many years later when I realized the lack of power in the word "try." The therapist threw his car keys on the floor and said, "Try to pick them up."

I looked at him oddly and thought:

TRY?

I didn't have to try to pick them up; I just had to do it! His point was well taken. I'd been using lame excuses and calling them reasons for not succeeding in my attempts to grow or accomplish something. Usually I was avoiding a fear of some kind.

There are rare occasions when the word 'try' is appropriate, but in personal growth, it usually doesn't apply. I finally found the courage to "do" more than try. I think I've done well.

Epilogue

I've spent nearly 30 years working on this manuscript. I've rewritten it and edited it at least seven times. Each time I finished, I realized that it wasn't really done. That's because I wasn't done either; I had so much more growing to do. I didn't have all the answers I needed for myself yet, never mind a book. The truth is, I may never have all those answers, but at least I'm growing.

These were the best years of my life in that I've healed throughout the repeated writings of this book along with an abundance of self-help study. I feel so nourished with the knowledge of life, its trials and tribulations, its rewards and glory. I look forward to tomorrow, next week, and next year. Each day I learn something that will help me move into the future with more confidence and wisdom. That's all I want from each day; something to learn that I can carry with me into all my tomorrows.

There's no doubt I was overwhelmed with a lot of horrible experiences in my life. When I was finally able to recognize, rise above, and use those experiences—good or bad—to learn and grow from them, I was able to learn to start living instead of just existing in misery. I don't mean to imply that my life experiences were trivial, but it happened and I can't change that. What I had to do was examine each damaging event, then recognize and understand the real effect it had on me. That was the only way I was going to truly understand myself and work toward overcoming the damage to the best of my ability.

I've often thought about my foster brother and sister and wonder what happened to them. I have tried to locate them without any success. The thought of their pain and suffering will always be a part of me.

The brother I grew up with and partly raised now only speaks to me when absolutely necessary. Our mother and his father, the man who raped me since I was a child, convinced him that I'm crazy. But they had a lot of time to do that since he was only 10 years old and very impressionable when I left home. Although he never experienced the abuse I did, it's obvious (to more than just me) that he didn't go unscathed by the lifestyle we grew up in either, but it isn't for me to examine.

My father often said most things are mind over matter. Many things—especially health—can be influenced by our state of mind, but I believed it was unequivocally true until I experienced an event in 2012 that caused my mind and body to completely shutdown.

I was at the gynecologist's office having an internal biopsy. The procedure was extremely uncomfortable, but the pain wasn't the prevailing issue. To be honest, I didn't know what it was, but my heart raced and I felt horrible all over. I guess I panicked and didn't really know why at the time. Then the doctor put some medicine on the spot where he'd taken the biopsy to help stop the bleeding.

The next thing I remember is hearing someone ask me, "Do you know where you are?"

I heard the voice again; I opened my eyes and saw a man's face looking down at me. I looked back at him and tried to figure out who he was. I knew him from somewhere, but I couldn't place where. I looked around the room and realized I was in a doctor's office, and it started coming back as to why I was there.

I was shaking and sweating profusely. The doctor asked me, "Do you have a history of seizures?"

I was still groggy. I closed my eyes for a moment as a rumble of anger rose in my gut, I shook my head and said, "Well, yeah… not exactly… it's a long story."

He asked me if I was going to be okay and I thought I was, but I wasn't. I could hardly function. Walking was difficult. I was weak and shaky, as if I'd gone into a severe sugar low. I had to take the biopsy to the hospital lab. I could hardly make it into the lobby. They admitted me immediately.

I explained what had happened to the doctor. I told him about my history of being severely abused and what they claimed were seizures. I told him I'd stopped taking my medications when I was in my mid-twenties and I thought the reaction—no matter how severe—was a result of being raped so brutally as a child. He agreed and decided it was better to make sure everything was okay by doing an abdominal CT scan. He didn't find anything abnormal there either.

Several hours passed. I rested a lot. By the time I went home, I felt fine physically, but mentally, I'd taken a hard blow.

I hadn't taken seizure medication in more than 20 years and I'd never had a problem until now. That was all the confirmation I needed to prove I didn't have epilepsy—ever—I'd just experienced the cause of my blackout. The pain from the procedure had evidently brought back memories of the painful sexual abuse with my stepfather and so many other men my mother had sold me to for sex when I was a little girl. I was angry with them all over again.

I talked to a dear friend about what had happened. He's also no stranger to abuse, so he speaks from experience. He told me some things would never go away—never. I know he's right, but I didn't like hearing it. I'd put a lot of faith in the mind over matter thing but had no control over this **body memory** and, if I ever feel that kind of pain again, I can't know that I wouldn't blackout again. That's just another one of those things I have to accept.

I'm blessed to have friends I can share these things with. I'm not ashamed of my life or my past—I used to be terribly ashamed—but there are still so many things that are difficult to talk about without shaking inside—and often on the outside.

That's another one of those things I don't think I'll ever conquer, but I'll never let it stop me from living.

Growing up for the first time at the age of 25 was difficult. A lot of my dysfunctional behaviors had become second nature, so it wasn't easy to break the pattern. I'd lived that way for so long, I didn't recognize that a lot of my problems even existed; that's the way I'd always been.

It's probably true that no one would have ever understood me the way my father did. He had more than just good life skills to help understand me; he also had the genetics. I'm like him in many good ways, and I know that helped him see through all the crap that disguised my true self.

I've dedicated so much time to turning my life story into a beneficial and helpful tool. I've watched my life blossom and it's because of this book. I desperately wanted to share it with other survivors like me. What I'd learned through the trials and errors of actually living through the process of healing was amazing. I needed to share what worked for me because the results were so effective.

I've often asked myself, Why I am so fortunate to have turned out so well while other survivors still suffer with their pasts with such agony? Today most people would never suspect that my life had so much turmoil. That's good, since I don't want to be a walking billboard in my personal or professional life.

In the end, it doesn't really matter where I came from and what kind of life I've had. What does matter is who I am today and how I conduct myself as a woman in this world. I think I've done well considering I stepped out of that isolated world into a world that was foreign to me and bravely worked and struggled to fit in. I didn't know what was right or acceptable, I wasn't sure of much of anything, but I learned. I finally had a choice and it was up to me to take advantage of that.

As I look back at the pictures of my youth, I want to remind you to never look at yourself today and not like what you see. Find what there is to like. Never look at yourself and wish you were better or more like someone else because one day you will look back and wonder why you lost so much of your past in ill feelings about yourself. For most of my young life I wished I were better or more like other people. I didn't think I was pretty and I didn't learn to like myself until it was too late to enjoy those days. Now middle-aged, I'm going to enjoy myself as best I can.

I have often wondered why I had to go through such hell. As I tell you this, I remember sitting on my bed the day I took all those pills and thinking how I felt like a failure because I couldn't even kill myself right.

THIS GOD PERSON MUST HAVE A PURPOSE FOR ME, A REASON FOR ME TO BE ALIVE. A REASON WHY I WAS GOING THROUGH ALL THIS CRAP. WHY? WHAT COULD IT BE? WHAT COULD I POSSIBLY DO FOR ANYONE? WHAT PURPOSE COULD I HAVE? WHAT GOOD AM I?

Within the pages of this book, I believe is the reason I survived—in order to share my life's lessons with you. Thank you for letting me share my life with you. I truly hope I have been able to offer you some benefit as a result of it—if so, thank your God—I was not alone throughout this project, nor was I driven by ambition alone.

By the way, a dear friend of mine brought it to my attention that my mother died exactly one year ago, to the day I finished this book.

Glossary of Terms

A

Adult Child of an Alcoholic:

These are the 14 Traits of an Adult Child of an Alcoholic according to ACoA, also known as the "The Laundry List."

1. We became isolated and afraid of people and authority figures.

2. We became approval seekers and lost our identity in the process.

3. We are frightened of angry people and any personal criticism.

4. We either become alcoholics, marry them or both, or find another compulsive personality such as a workaholic to fulfill our sick abandonment needs.

5. We live life from the viewpoint of victims and we are attracted by that weakness in our love and friendship relationships.

6. We have an overdeveloped sense of responsibility and it is easier for us to be concerned with others rather than ourselves; this enables us not to look too closely at our own faults, etc.

7. We get guilt feelings when we stand up for ourselves instead of giving in to others.

8. We became addicted to excitement.

9. We confuse love and pity and tend to "love" people we can "pity" and "rescue."

10. We have "stuffed" our feelings from our traumatic childhoods and have lost the ability to feel or express our feelings because it hurts so much (Denial).

11. We judge ourselves harshly and have a very low sense of self-esteem.

12. We are dependent personalities who are terrified of abandonment and will do anything to hold on to a relationship in order not to experience painful abandonment feelings, which we received from living with sick people who were never there emotionally for us.

13. Alcoholism is a family disease; and we became para-alcoholics and took on the characteristics of that disease even though we did not pick up the drink.

14. Para-alcoholics are reactors rather than actors. - ACoA (Adult Children of Alcoholics)

B

Body memory:

Body memory is a sensorimotor function which can be suppressed if the experience is traumatic, but it can be reawakened when faced with a similar event. - Psychology Dictionary

Bottle club:

A member's club where people can drink after the closing hours allowed by law at a public bar. Members will buy their alcohol by the bottle either at the time or in advance.

C

Co-dependent:

The History Behind the Concept of Codependency by Diane England, Ph. D.:

Originally, the concept of codependency was developed and used by those in the recovery field (recovery from alcoholism, that is) to refer to the type of beliefs and behaviors that adults who grew up in families impacted by alcohol typically exhibited. In other words, adult children of alcoholics often held some similar dysfunctional beliefs, and they displayed some similar maladaptive behaviors. But then, as children, they were basically forced into adopting certain beliefs and behaviors because parents or caregivers demanded this of them. Then again, these beliefs or behaviors may have helped these children to better cope with their chaotic home lives, including helping them to minimize some of the emotional and physical pain that was often a part of it.

In time, therapists and others realized that more than children of alcoholics displayed some of these same dysfunctional beliefs and behaviors. Other problems besides alcoholism that created such self-defeating beliefs and behaviors in adults included:

Other forms of chemical dependency in the family

➢ A family member with a chronic mental illness or physical illness

➢ Emotional abuse, verbal abuse, psychological abuse, mental abuse, physical abuse, and/or sexual abuse

➢ Hypercritical or overly demanding parents who expected more than a child was developmentally capable of delivering

➢ Neglect of a child's physical and/or emotional needs

➢ A rigid and unloving family environment

➢ Rigid family rules

➢ Family secrets that children knew but weren't allowed to divulge

➢ Obvious discord between the parents because of affairs or other problems

➢ Disruption from divorce.

Raised in such a household, a child develops behaviors which assist with survival in that dysfunctional family of origin. But as an adult, these same kinds of behaviors become maladaptive. In fact, they usually get in the person's way of getting needs met. And even though the individual may realize that these behaviors aren't in his or her best interest, the person engages in them, nonetheless. Thus, the woman who hid in her room to avoid the wrath of her alcoholic and abusive father, for example, may be comfortable hiding out from her alcoholic and abusive husband because this is familiar behavior from her childhood. Furthermore, the fear or anxiety she feels is familiar. But of course, this isn't what she truly wants for her life or from her relationship. While she desires a loving partnership, she is not going to be able to create one as long as her partner is abusing both alcohol and her.

Those who write about the codependent and codependency often talk about how codependents have unhealthy personal boundaries. Yes, those suffering from codependency are inclined to let others walk all over them. A codependent woman will likely try to cater to her addicted husband's every need despite the fact she receives little in return besides his emotional abuse and verbal abuse—if not worse. Meanwhile, of course, she ignores her own needs and wants.

Interestingly enough, though, codependents are hardly aware of their own needs or wants anyway. They are too used to turning outward and catering to what others and the environment demands of them. They are also out of touch with what they need and desire because they typically have a fragile sense of self. In fact, codependents often look to a partner, their roles, and/or a lifestyle for a sense of identity. However, living with an addicted and likely emotionally and verbally abusive partner only further erodes that fragile sense of self.

The codependent woman also lacks healthy personal boundaries--as demonstrated by her willingness to become enmeshed with her addicted partner and his addiction-related problems. An emotionally healthy woman would likely not hook up with someone with such problems in the first place. And, if he developed them after they were together, if she realized that he was not making any effort to take care of his problems, she would likely elect to leave the relationship. Indeed, she would not assume responsibility for everything that was going wrong--as the codependent woman is inclined to do.

Of course, dealing with all the drama and essentially becoming a martyr can provide a sense of purpose as well as feelings of noble accomplishment to a woman who is an expert at pleasing others--not herself. Since she doesn't know how to step forth and take a chance on pursuing actions or activities that may please her alone--because to do so may make her feel out of control--the codependent woman settles for her partner's addictions and abuse. Furthermore, she may settle for this destructive way of life because she doesn't believe that she is capable of making it on her own.

Comfort zone:

A psychological state in which a person feels familiar, at ease, in control, and experiences low anxiety. A person in this state uses a limited set of behaviors to deliver a steady level of performance, usually without a sense of risk. - Wikipedia

I'd like to add that when a fearful person, such as I was, is out of their comfort zone, I used a multitude of behaviors to survive emotionally. Most often, those behaviors were controlling or defensive. – Darlene Deacon

Conditional love:

The best way I can describe it is by using the word "conditional" meaning, "dependent upon." As long as I was acting within whatever my mother felt was appropriate at that moment, then she loved me. That could change in seconds depending upon what might be going on in her mind or how she might perceive something at the time.

Conscience:

The sense or consciousness of the moral goodness or blameworthiness of one's own conduct, intentions, or character together with a feeling of obligation to do right or be good – Merriam Webster

Corrupted fulfillment:

I have personally noticed that many emotionally insecure, depressed and spiritually empty people have children in an attempt to fill that void or cure the depression. That sets the parent up for a huge letdown because it doesn't work. The parent will often feel resentment toward the child which can lead to abuse and neglect. Conversely, the child is often facing a long, hard life of trying to accomplish the impossible—fill the psychological void in their parents. In my case, I learned to try to fill my mother's emotional needs. As the first-born child, that became my primary role in life. – Darlene Deacon

E

Electroencephalography:

Typically a non-invasive (however invasive electrodes are often used in specific applications) method to record electrical activity of the brain along the scalp. EEG measures voltage fluctuations resulting from ionic current within the neurons of the brain. – WikipediA

Enabler:

Codependent/Enabler/Caretaker - steps up and takes control if the alcoholic loses power - enabling is anything that protects the chemically dependent person from the consequences of their actions - spouse often takes on the role, but children and siblings can also be enablers (multigenerational alcoholic families will sometimes designate a child in this role, a sign of more serious pathology) - tends to everyone's needs in the family - loses sense of self in tasks of a domestic nature - never takes the time to assess his/her own needs and feelings - person never gains what they need most in order to get better: insight - never are confronted with the facts that would drive home the point: drugs or alcohol are destroying their lives and their family - as long as the enabler and the chemically dependent family members play their game of mutual self-deception, things never get better - they get worse - others cannot bond with the Caretaker due to the bustle of activity - The Caretaker's purpose: to maintain appropriate appearances to the outside world. - soberrecovery.com

Endometriosis:

The presence and growth of functioning endometrial tissue in places other than the uterus that often results in severe pain and infertility. – Merriam-Webster – Also, research from Harvard University has shown that women who report child sexual and physical abuse have a greater risk of being diagnosed with endometriosis in later life.

F

Fight or Flight Response:

The fight-or-flight response (also called the fight, flight, freeze, or fawn response [in PTSD], hyperarousal, or the acute stress response) is a physiological reaction that occurs in response to a perceived harmful event, attack, or threat to survival. It was first described by Walter Bradford Cannon. His theory states that animals react to threats with a general discharge of the sympathetic nervous system, priming the animal for fighting or fleeing. - WikipediA

G

Grooming:

Child grooming refers to actions deliberately undertaken with the aim of befriending and establishing an emotional connection with a child, to lower the child's inhibitions in preparation for sexual activity with the child, or exploitation. - Abuse Wiki

M

Minimize abuse:

Abused children will often minimize their abuse to a degree that makes it acceptable enough to endure. It's purely to protect ourselves from overwhelming fear. Admitting that the people we depend on for life, love, and protection could hurt us so horribly, would be too much for a child to bear. – Somewhere in my therapy – Darlene Deacon

N

Narcissistic with Sociopathic Tendencies:

Grandiosity, lack of conscience, ruthlessness, lack of empathy, deception and manipulation have become tools rather than bad character traits. This is especially the case with sociopathic narcissists--those individuals who have the narcissistic personality structure and also share many characteristics of the sociopath. These traits include a careless disregard for other human beings, including chronic extreme verbal abuse and stress perpetrated upon spouses and children. Sociopathic narcissists purposely seek out ways to delude and control those who will profit them materially, socially and professionally. They are gifted at leaving others "holding the bag" while they abscond with the profits of some else's labors. Leaving another person's life in shambles or even their entire family is of no concern or interest to the sociopathic narcissist who has adroitly moved ahead to his/her next cycle of acquisition and control. - Linda Martinez-Lewi, Ph.D.

Narcissistic Personality Disorder and Borderline Personality Disorder:

There is no specific single medical test (e.g., blood test) to diagnose BPD and a diagnosis is not based on a single sign or symptom. Rather, BPD is diagnosed by a mental health professional based on sustained patterns of thinking and behavior in an individual. Some people may have "borderline personality traits" which means that they do not meet criteria for diagnosis with BPD but have some of the symptoms associated with this illness.

Individuals with BPD usually have several of the following symptoms, many of which are detailed in the DSM-IV-TR:

> Marked mood swings with periods of intense depressed mood, irritability and/or anxiety lasting a few hours to a few days (but not

in the context of a full-blown episode of major depressive disorder or bipolar disorder).

➤ Inappropriate, intense or uncontrollable anger.

➤ Impulsive behaviors that result in adverse outcomes and psychological distress, such as excessive spending, sexual encounters, substance use, shoplifting, reckless driving or binge eating.

➤ Recurring suicidal threats or non-suicidal self-injurious behavior, such as cutting or burning one's self.

➤ Unstable, intense personal relationships, sometimes alternating between "all good," idealization, and "all bad," devaluation.

➤ Persistent uncertainty about self-image, long-term goals, friendships and values.

➤ Chronic boredom or feelings of emptiness.

➤ Frantic efforts to avoid abandonment.

Borderline personality disorder is relatively common—about 1 in 20 or 25 individuals will live with this condition. Historically, BPD has been thought to be significantly more common in females, however recent research suggests that males may be almost as frequently affected by BPD. Borderline personality disorder is diagnosed in people from each race, ethnicity and economic status.

The two personality disorders even have a rate of co-occurrence of about 25 percent - National Alliance on Mental Illness (NAMI)

P

Psychogenic Non-epileptic Seizures:

A PNES is a seizure-like event that is produced, not by abnormal electrical charges in the brain, but by psychological factors of which the patient is not fully aware and cannot control. Psychogenic non-epileptic seizures go by many names, including pseudoseizures, psychological seizures, psychosomatic seizures, psychogenic seizures. - Robert S. Fisher, M.D., Ph.D., Maslah Saul MD Professor of Neurology, Stanford

R

Roles in Dysfunctional Families by Robert Burney M.A. - author, counselor, and a pioneer in the field of inner child healing / codependency recovery.

(This is a full list ((since some are not included in my story)) for those of you who may be able to relate to one or more of them. — Darlene Deacon)

"We have come to understand that both the passive and the aggressive behavioral defense systems are reactions to the same kinds of childhood trauma, to the same kinds of emotional wounds. The Family Systems Dynamics research shows that within the family system, children adopt certain roles according to their family dynamics. Some of these roles are more passive, some are more aggressive, because in the competition for attention and validation within a family system the children must adopt different types of behaviors in order to feel like an individual."

The emotional dynamics of dysfunctional families are basic - and like emotional dynamics for all human beings are pretty predictable. The outside details may look quite different due to a variety of factors, but the dynamics of the human emotional process are the same for all human beings everywhere.

The basic roles which I list below apply to American culture specifically, and Western Civilization generally - but with a few changes in details could be made to fit most any culture.

There are four basic roles that children adopt in order to survive growing up in emotionally dishonest, shame-based, dysfunctional family systems. Some children maintain one role into adulthood while others switch from one role to another as the family dynamic changes (i.e. when the oldest leaves home, etc.) An only child may play all of the roles at one time or another.

"Responsible Child" - "Family Hero"

This is the child who is "9 going on 40." This child takes over the parent role at a very young age, becoming very responsible and self-sufficient. They give the family self-worth because they look good on the outside. They are the good students, the sports stars, the prom queens. The parents look to this child to prove that they are good parents and good people.

As an adult, the Family Hero is rigid, controlling, and extremely judgmental (although perhaps very subtle about it) - of others and secretly of themselves. They achieve "success" on the outside and get lots of positive attention but are cut off from their inner emotional life, from their True Self. They are compulsive and driven as adults because deep inside they feel inadequate and insecure.

The family hero, because of their "success" in conforming to dysfunctional cultural definitions of what constitutes doing life "right", is often the child in the family who as an adult has the hardest time even admitting that there is anything within themselves that needs to be healed.

"Acting out child" - "Scapegoat"

This is the child that the family feels ashamed of - and the most emotionally honest child in the family. He/she acts out the tension and anger the family ignores. This child provides distraction from the real issues in the family. The scapegoat usually has trouble in school because they get attention the only way they know how - which is negatively. They often become pregnant or addicted as teenagers.

These children are usually the most sensitive and caring which is why they feel such tremendous hurt. They are romantics who become very cynical and distrustful. They have a lot of self-hatred and can be very self-destructive. This often results in this child becoming the first person in the family to get into some kind of recovery.

For a more, in-depth explanation see "Scapegoat" under "S" in this Glossary.

"Placater " - "Mascot" - "Caretaker":

This child takes responsibility for the emotional well-being of the family. They become the families 'social director' and/or clown, diverting the family's attention from the pain and anger.

This child becomes an adult who is valued for their kind heart, generosity, and ability to listen to others. Their whole self-definition is centered on others and they don't know how to get their own needs met. They become adults who cannot receive love, only give it. They often have case loads rather than friendships - and get involved in abusive relationships in an attempt to "save" the other person They go into the helping professions and become nurses, and social workers, and therapists. They have very low self-worth and feel a lot of guilt that they work very hard to overcome by being really "nice" (i.e. people pleasing, classically codependent) people.

"Adjuster" - "Lost Child:"

This child escapes by attempting to be invisible. They daydream, fantasize, read a lot of books or watch a lot of TV. They deal with reality by withdrawing from it. They deny that they have any feelings and "don't bother getting upset."

These children grow up to be adults who find themselves unable to feel and suffer very low self-esteem. They are terrified of intimacy and often have relationship phobia. They are very withdrawn and shy and become socially isolated because that is the only way they know to be safe from being hurt. A lot of actors and writers are 'lost children' who have found a way to express emotions while hiding behind their characters.

S

Scapegoat:

Here is another, more in-depth explanation of 'Scapegoat' by Andrea Mathews, L.P.C., a Cognitive and Transpersonal Therapist I wanted to add because it gives so much more detail and understanding of the role.

The role of the child who is designated as the family scapegoat in dysfunctional families is to serve as the identified "problem" in the family. Also known as the family's "black sheep," the child who is given this role tends to be the focus of the family. The family can point to the child who is placed in the role as the scapegoat and blame the family's problems on this child, which is the primary reason why families designate a particular child, usually the most vulnerable one, to be in this role.

According to Andrea Mathews, L.P.C., a Cognitive and Transpersonal Therapist, as a naturally sensitive or empathic child grows up in the home with parents and others who cannot be "wrong," who blame the child for things they themselves have done or who otherwise refuse to take responsibility for their own inner lives, the child may begin to empathize with, then carry, then identify with all of the unresolved flotsam and jetsam floating around in this home. Sensitive and empathic children--not having been taught how to use empathy--can be used by family, whether intentionally or unintentionally, as the carrier of the "sins" of the family. Children are seeking mirrors, as we've said in other blogs, that define them. If the only mirror is one that defines the child as the guilty party or the responsible one, a sensitive child, who longs for connection, will begin to define him or herself accordingly.

As that child grows he will encounter more and more of the world, but will come from the same exact dynamic established at home. Why? Because he has identified with this way of interacting. He thinks it's who he is. He is the guilty one. The one who must constantly take responsibility for others emotions and "sins" because this is just what he does. He cares a great deal for others--as a natural part of his authenticity--but this caring has been contorted, by this defined identity, into carrying.

So now, this child, whose gift it was to be empathic, has now been cursed. She will not use her empathy as recognition of what others are feeling, and the ability to mirror that back to them so that they can then use that information for their own growth. She will use her gift of empathy to carry other's burdens of guilt, responsibility and emotion. And in so doing, she will somehow prove to herself that she is not the bad person she senses that she is.

This sense of unworthiness carried deep within and below every good deed done by the Scapegoat originates from having carried the guilt and responsibility for others' "sins." This child has taken on these "wrongs" and "sins" as if they should, indeed, belong to him. And he feels this sense of wrongness as if it actually defines him. He is now, officially the Scapegoat--for he has taken the "sins" of others away.

Self-esteem:

A confidence and satisfaction in oneself - self-respect – Merriam Webster

Self-respect:

1: a proper respect for oneself as a human being

2: regard for one's own standing or position – Merriam Webster

Stockholm Syndrome:

The Stockholm Syndrome was originally developed to explain the phenomenon of hostages bonding with their captors. The name refers to a bank holdup in Stockholm, Sweden in 1973 when four people were held hostage for six days by two men. The hostages and their captors bonded with each other and the hostages actually came to see their captors as protecting them from the police. One was even reported as later becoming engaged to one of the captors.

Subsequent research found that such a reaction had occurred in all the "hostage" groups studied, including cult members, battered women, incest victims and physically or emotionally abused children. Researchers have concluded that this seems to be a universal phenomenon which may be instinctive and thus play a survival function for hostages who are victims of abuse.

There is no universally accepted definition of the Stockholm Syndrome but it has been suggested that it is present if one or more of the following is observed:

➢ Positive feelings by the captive towards his/her captor.

- ➢ Negative feelings by the captive toward the police or authorities trying to win his/her release.
- ➢ Positive feelings by the captor towards his/her captive.

It has been found to occur in circumstances where there is:

- ➢ A perceived threat to survival and a belief that the captor is willing to carry out that threat.
- ➢ A perception by the captive of some small kindness from the captor within the context of terror.
- ➢ Isolation from perspectives other than those of the captor.
- ➢ Perceived inability to escape.

The following explanation has been put forward for the phenomenon.

The abuser (or captor) terrifies the victim, who cannot escape, by threatening his or her physical or psychological survival. As a result of being terrified the victim needs nurturance and protection. Being isolated from others, the victim must turn to the abuser for this if s/he turns to anyone. If the abuser shows the victim some small kindness this creates hope in the victim, who then ignores her rage at the terror-creating side of the abuser (because this rage would be experienced as overwhelming) and bonds to the positive side of the abuser. With the hope that the abuser will let him or her live, the victim works to keep the abuser happy. In trying to determine what will keep the abuser happy, the victim's own needs, feelings and perspectives must take second place and s/he unconsciously takes on the world view of the abuser. The victim sees the abuser as the "good guy" and those trying to win his/her release (e.g. police or therapists) as the "bad guys", as this is the way the abuser sees things. Over a period of months or years, the victim's entire sense of self may come to be experienced through the eyes of the abuser. The victim may have extreme difficulty leaving the abuser, if the opportunity arises, because s/he no longer sees a reason to do so.

For victims of sexual abuse, their families and therapists, the Stockholm Syndrome is useful in explaining the victim's experiences, current "symptoms" and the relationship between victim and abuser. It can help remove the tendency of the victim to blame him or herself for "allowing" the abuse to continue or for "causing" the abuse. It can also help to make sense of the ways in which the victim's perceptions of themselves and the abuser can be distorted, by explaining those distortions in terms of the Syndrome and making clear their origins as an instinctive survival function.

The following are some common ways in which the victim's view of their situation can become distorted, with the corresponding explanations in terms of the Stockholm Syndrome:

➢ The victim denies the abuser's violence against him/her and focuses on his positive side.

➢ Explanation: An unconscious attempt to find hope (and thus a way to survive) in a situation in which s/he would otherwise feel powerless and overwhelmed.

➢ The victim feels shame for abuse done to him/her.

➢ Explanation: Reflects the victim having taken the abuser's perspective (namely, that s/he caused the abuse and therefore it was deserved).

➢ The victim resents outsiders' attempts to free him/her from the abuser.

➢ Explanation: The victim knows that the abuser is likely to retaliate against him/her for any disloyalty shown, so s/he resists others' attempts to free her or to hold the abuser accountable for the abuse.

➢ The victim identifies with the "victim" in the abuser.

- ➢ Explanation: This represents the projection of the victim's own victim status onto the abuser. It enables the victim to feel sympathetic and caring towards the abuser.
- ➢ The victim believes s/he deserved the abuser's violence.
- ➢ Explanation: This represents an attempt to feel that s/he controls when and whether the violence/abuse is done and thus permits him/her to believe s/he can stop the abuse.
- ➢ The victim rationalizes the abuser's violence against him/her.
- ➢ Explanation: An attempt to maintain a bond with the abuser (and thus hope of survival) in the face of behavior (abuse) that would otherwise destroy that bond (hope).
- ➢ Victim uses abuser-as-victim explanation to account for the abuse.
- ➢ Explanation: This represents an effort to see the abuser in a positive light so as to maintain the bond (since the bond provides the victim with the only hope of surviving).
- ➢ The victim feels hatred for that part of him/her which the abuser said led to the abuse.
- ➢ Explanation: To improve chances of survival, the victim internalizes the abuser's perspective, including the reasons given for the abuse.
- ➢ The victim fears the abuser will come to get him/her, even if he is dead or in prison.

Explanation: The victim knows the abuser is willing to "get" him/her because he has done so at least once before. The victim remains loyal in anticipation of his return. - The South Eastern Centre Against Sexual Assault (SECASA)

Index

Personality Disorder, 162, 181

Narcissistic with Sociopathic Tendencies, 162, 181

Roles in Dysfunctional Families, 60, 183–85

Worthy Quote

THERAPY ONLY HELPS US WHEN WE HAVE A GENUINE DESIRE TO KNOW OURSELVES AS WE REALLY ARE... BUT IT DOES LITTLE GOOD IF WE ONLY WANT TO KNOW WHO WE WOULD LIKE TO BE.

FROM THE SERIES, "HANNIBAL."

About the Author

Being a survivor of horrific child abuse, Darlene is working to create new legislation that would better prosecute child predators and improve protection for victims.

Darlene Deacon worked as a news reporter at KIDK-TV—a CBS affiliate—in Idaho Falls, Idaho. She primarily covered crime and investigative pieces, but she also enjoyed the more technical stories at the Idaho National Laboratory (the nation's premier nuclear science and technology lab) as the special reporter. She later produced the six & ten pm news for KIDK.

She got her start in television news as a copywriter at FOX's WSVN-TV Channel 7 in Miami where she was as a newscast copy writer.

Deacon studied broadcasting at the Connecticut School of Broadcasting in North Palm Beach, Florida, and creative writing at Broward Community College.

Darlene is also a character actress and a member of the Screen Actors Guild. She has appeared in several television productions. Her past credits include a co-starring role in a FOX television series called "Super Force" and had a small part in a movie made for USA Network television entitled "Red Wind." Darlene has performed in a number of other films and television shows.

Darlene was born in Waltham, Massachusetts and grew up in logging country in Maine. She says with a smile on her face, "They took away my ballet shoes and handed me an axe when I was nine."

If you would like to contact the author, email her at: darlene@darlenedeacon.com

Made in United States
Troutdale, OR
02/04/2025